Peace Beyond Belief

Transcending Your World
From the Inside Out

Donna Lee Humble

Copyright © 2024 ShaneLise Publishing

All rights reserved. No part of this book may be reproduced in any form without permission in writing from the publisher, except in the case of brief quotations embodied in critical articles or reviews.

All quotes are from A Course in Miracles, copyright ©2007 by the Foundation for Inner Peace, copyright holder and publisher, 448 Ignacio Blvd., #306, Novato, CA 94949, acim.org, used with permission.

Edited by Erin E. Kannon
Back cover photo by Orange Fox Photography
ISBN: 978-1-7372626-3-3

Dedication

To Billy, whose adventurous spirit is alive in me now and forever.

I'm thrilled to share a few thoughts on Donna Lee Humble's insightful book, *Peace Beyond Belief*. As someone who has spent years exploring and teaching the principles of Soul Recovery, I find Donna Lee's insights to be both powerful and deeply resonant with the work I do.

In *Peace Beyond Belief*, Donna Lee opens up about her own experiences with trauma and adversity, showing us how true healing involves being curious about the root of our suffering. She explains how our perceptions, beliefs, and thought patterns often lie at the heart of our pain. What I love about this book is how Donna Lee makes it clear that healing is a profoundly spiritual process. She teaches us to look beyond the surface and recognize the stories we create about ourselves and our lives, encouraging us to embrace our difficult emotions instead of avoiding them.

Donna Lee's journey through various spiritual practices, including the spiritual psychotherapy from *A Course in Miracles*, provides a rich foundation for her message of hope and healing. She gently guides readers to let go of limiting beliefs, practice forgiveness, and find a deep sense of inner peace that can carry us through life's challenges. Her approach aligns beautifully with the principles of Soul Recovery, making this book a perfect companion for anyone on a spiritual path.

Peace Beyond Belief is more than just a book—it's a guide to understanding ourselves better and finding peace within. Donna Lee's wisdom and honesty shine through every page, offering practical advice and heartfelt encouragement.

I highly recommend *Peace Beyond Belief* to anyone looking to heal and grow. Donna Lee Humble's words are sure to inspire and uplift you, just as they have for me and so many others.

Warmly,

Rev. Rachel Harrison

Spiritual Coach and Host of the Recover Your Soul Podcast

When life has taken its toll, sometimes a thoughtful guide with a kind heart is the healing salve to get us through. Donna Lee Humble gifts a grounding reset worthy of a familiar corner on your nightstand. Richly curated with practical purpose, *Peace Beyond Belief* delivers with heart and integrity. Inspired by enduring faith and Humble's holistic wellness practice, you'll find these pages a welcome friend along your journey across the emotional, intellectual, and spiritual landscape of personal reflection.

Evan Zislis

Author, *ClutterFree Revolution: Simplify Your Stuff, Organize Your Life & Save the World*

Donna Lee vulnerably shares how she has overcome and transformed traumatic events in her life, using them as catalysts to connect to her higher self. Her journey is proof that we have the ability to heal ourselves and can ultimately connect to the goodness and truth of who we truly are. She teaches that true power lies in shifting our perceptions and letting go of ego. Donna Lee beautifully weaves lessons from *A Course in Miracles* with her own experiences, allowing the reader to see its applications in action. Her story is an inspiration to anyone on a journey of self-healing and spiritual expansion.

Best,

Ashley Mauldin

Licensed Therapist and Founder of Daring Women

Table of Contents

Acknowledgments 1

Foreword 3

Introduction 9

Part I: Crashing Waves 19
   Chapter 1: Humble Beginnings 21
   Chapter 2: Strange Dreams 37
   Chapter 3: Tossed Like a Cork 49
   Chapter 4: The Robbers Too 57
   Chapter 5: Good Grief 67

Part II: You Cannot Hide 75
   Chapter 6: She's Come Undone 77
   Chapter 7: What's Normal Anyway? 91
   Chapter 8: Not an Ideal World 99
   Chapter 9: Fix or Forgive 105
   Chapter 10: The Master Within 115
   Chapter 11: A Delicate Subject 119
   Chapter 12: A Direct Route 127
   Chapter 13: Lost in Thought 135
   Chapter 14: Riding the Rollercoaster 147

Chapter 15: Prison or Passageway 157

Part III: Undoing the Madness 169

Chapter 16: The Only Way Out 171
Chapter 17: The Rabbit Hole 179
Chapter 18: Into Fear or Into Flow 187
Chapter 19: Playing With Fire 193
Chapter 20: The Trappings of the Small Mind 205
Chapter 21: Dust in the Wind 213
Chapter 22: Your Best Interest 219
Chapter 23: If It's Not One Thing 225

Part IV: Tranquil Seas 229

Chapter 24: Yet Another Clever Disguise 231
Chapter 25: Steeped in Joy and Devotion 239
Chapter 26: Life Is Pretty Amazing 247
Chapter 27: Mastering the River of Life 255

Bibliography 261

About the Author 263

Acknowledgments

Every being who walked through the pages of my life—whether I saw you as a bad guy or a saint—I learned from each of you.

Though my little brother Billy inspired the writing of this book, I thank my sisters Jackie, whose dynamic, witty, fun-loving spirit remains with all of us, and Pamela, who stuck around through the good and the ugly, always there to help any family member in need and provide the glue that keeps us together. Mom and Dad, for your love and laughter and for providing a family unit as best you could for as long as you could. Of course, my children—Jeremy, for your bright enthusiasm, expanding my vocabulary, and offering remarkable insights, and Jacinda, for your objective practical encouragement, teaching me to map my ideas, and agreeing to set goals together for our books. No one could have inspired me more than the two of you in your own unique and beautiful ways.

To my first therapist, Tom Hill, who taught me to meditate so many years ago. The 12 Steps of AA and all of the members who reminded me that in our weakness will we find our strength. The fresh, spiritually expanding concepts of *A Course in Miracles* that showed up in that tiny book by Gerald Jampolsky more than four decades ago. Jesus Christ, for appearing in my darkest moments to prove to me there is so much beyond the physical. To all who attended our local *A*

Course in Miracles meetings—it was through your experiences, questions, and compassion for each other that I grew spiritually by applying this philosophy to my world, which set the stage to eventually put them in written form. To Ericka Anderson, for your skilled approach to EMDR and unwavering patience as I worked through past trauma.

My husband, Dwayne, for being my best teacher and for your patience and willingness to explore ways to improve our marriage. And for encouraging me and sometimes just giving me space all the way through the writing and publishing process of yet another book. And most of all, for the hours you gave listening to me read out loud every page and thoughtfully making simple, sensible, and applicable suggestions to perfect this book.

Thank you, Erin Kannon, for your masterful editing skills and for coming on board with me for the second time. I'm grateful you were available. Thank you, Nicollette Halladay, for steering me in the right direction and acting as my cheerleader while both prudently and effectively helping me land speaking gigs and get my books in the hands of those who were receptive to the message and ready to up-level their lives.

How lucky I've been for all who have shown up in the perfect timing. Without each of you, this book would have remained somewhere floating around in the ethers.

Foreword

Two of my favorite books are *A Return to Love* by Marianne Williamson and *A Course in Miracles Made Easy* by Alan Cohen. Now, Donna Lee Humble has written *Peace Beyond Belief*, another favorite that will rest along with these two on my nightstand for ongoing support, guidance, and inspiration guided by *A Course in Miracles*.

I am known for promoting health, wellness, and inspirational authors, including Marianne, Alan, and Donna Lee, with my magazines and speaker series. The interesting thing about my purpose to provide resources for my readers to heal and grow into the best versions of themselves is that I have experienced a profound transformation in spending time and having sessions with our contributors, including Donna Lee. Her sessions, like this book, take us on a journey from our childhood wounds to peace beyond belief.

The riveting beginning of the book, as Donna Lee shares her childhood trauma, was so shockingly similar to mine that it perfectly revealed how fear and chaos are imprinted on our psyche and how they affect our functionality, inhibiting our ability to love ourselves and others.

We are living in a time of great change. We are being forced by the Universe to grow or go. There seems to be no other choice. If you are ready to choose growth, stop avoiding the uncomfortable emotions that are subconsciously driving your life. If you are ready to find peace and love, this book can be your guide. If you are in an existential crisis as I was when I walked into Donna Lee's office after a divorce that shattered my ego, as she identifies in the following pages, and my attachment to the external life I had lost, with the small self keeping me stuck and preventing me from living a fully expressed life, her words are for you.

In her book *Seek, Not for Love*, Donna Lee guided us inward. In *Peace Beyond Belief,* she not only takes us deeper into ourselves but shares *how* to get there with meditation, changing our thoughts and beliefs, our perceptions. You can feel she is on a mission to help set us free from the inner pain that causes our external dysfunctional patterns. Her book is a guide to inner peace that will calm the external and transform our dysfunctional lives into miraculous living.

Are you seeking relief? Are you ready to stop running from your uncomfortable feelings? The pain we run from is our gateway to the freedom and peace we seek. This book will take you from the trauma that binds you to the healing depths of meditation, along with Donna Lee's use of *A Course in Miracles*. If we do not break our patterns, our patterns will break us. Whether we wait for the tower moment that brings us to our knees or we voluntarily seek growth, the opportunity is ours. When my husband filed for divorce in 2020, my first thought was, "Okay, this is an opportunity for transformation." Intuitively, I knew I was going to lean into the pain and allow it to transform me. Did I know how difficult it would be? No. Did I know it would take four years to clear out my feelings of rejection, abandonment, and inadequacy. No. I signed the divorce papers and holed up in a cabin for a month, feeling and healing. I reached for resources like Donna Lee and books like this to soothe my transformation, which felt like a mutation in the movie *Alien*. I know people prefer the chrysalis and the butterfly analogy, but let's be real—it can feel more like *Alien*, and it can feel just as terrifying.

Breaking the patterns, feeling our pain, changing our thought patterns, and forgiving ourselves and others is the journey you are about to embark on in this book. The result will be your freedom, peace, and glow-up! I can promise if you stay the course with Donna Lee's guidance, you will not only feel better emotionally but also transform physically into that gorgeous butterfly. You will be the goddess and god that you truly came here to be. You will be more authentic, empowered, and successful in your divine purpose. You will find your divine purpose, and most of all, you will find love and peace beyond belief.

Stacy Oliver, President of Soul Stream Media

Publisher of *Mind Body Soul* magazine, *The Healthy Planet*, and *Yoga & Spa* magazine

Director of The Extraordinary People Lecture Series and the Live Your Power Expo & Speaker Summits

Who looks outside, dreams; who looks inside, awakes.

—Carl Jung

Introduction

"When you believe something, you have made it true for you."

—*A Course in Miracles* (T-7.VI.7:7-8)

It's happening again. I've planted pen and paper by my bed, in the car, and everywhere else I can think of, for I am waking in the early hours and often while driving jolted by words streaming through. Words that must find an outlet on paper to such a point that I would fear if I didn't write them down that instant they would be lost forever. However, without exception, they would somehow come back when I sat in front of my manuscript, or I'd discover that I had already written them in my notes. That proved to me this was another opportunity to serve a greater purpose. I was convinced these words must be expressed and known, having a meeting place for you and me where Spirit longs to know itself. Words may be only symbols, yet they have more power than we can imagine. Power to comfort, to connect, to inspire, and to heal, especially when they touch the heart and especially when they reveal our oneness.

This time, it's coming in pieces like an immense jigsaw puzzle that, as it finally came together, depicted my essence as if I were holding a tiger by the tail. Ha ha! Eighteen months ago, I tried to silence the call, but trying to push it away only made it come out sideways, backsliding slowly into old tendencies which I thought I'd overcome. Ultimately, I prayed:

> "Thank you, Great Spirit, for your patience in finally allowing myself to hear You directing me to write again. I heard You asking me to touch the lives of my fellow light travelers. Please remove from me the doubts, fear of being pompous or not being good enough so that I may do Your will. Please work through me in the way that serves my sisters and brothers and our purpose of oneness. How do I turn around the perceived atrocities to aid those seeking a higher path and help to bring them through imagined shock to peace? How do I lead them there without harming them?"

As I asked this I was instantly reminded that we cannot be hurt but by our own thoughts. Oh, yeah!

How do I overcome fatigue, so tired, so unmotivated, so doubtful and unconfident in my abilities? Weeks later, the light bulb flipped on, and I was reminded I was not writing this book. To let go of the ego and merely channel Great Spirit's wish to communicate with you through this book. And so here we are meeting again on paper.

You must be one of them. Those few who are ready to dig deep to rediscover the peace that you know is in there. Congratulations for daring to dive deeper.

This book is for those who have been there, done that. Those who have been through hard times and come out the other side yet continue to meet with struggle and hit various walls in their lives and in their minds. All the work they've done has left them still wanting and feeling lost, exposing a bottomless pit of dissatisfaction.

After decades of self-improvement you find yourself in "no man/woman's land." Just this side of the flow, the effortlessness, lasting joy, and inner peace that you intuit is there just beyond your grasp. You may not be asking for Nirvana—you just want a safe, stable, purposeful, happy existence. Yet you are plagued with a distant knowing that something is still missing. This cannot be it! It feels like reaching a false summit after years only to find the true summit is still well beyond your capacity or your sight. *Why did I put in all the work*, you may exclaim!

Are you at a crossroads too? The words that follow are for those who've come through misfortune and tough times, ready to up-level their lives, spiritually driven to finally reconcile all that blocks their ability to love *freely and joyously.*

This book was written especially for you if you consider yourself a spiritual seeker. You may be looking for meaning beyond navigating the physical world that we live in yet find yourself caught in a net of earthly demands that keep you forever driving and striving.

Who hasn't had a traumatic event in their life, a major loss, or a series of repetitive disappointments? We get stuck in the shock of it all, blaming others, the "system," our parents, or God. Right? We go from anger to fear to guilt. We spend our lives clamoring for superiority on one end or outrunning feelings of inferiority on the other. Yearning, lusting for more or better, toward swinging the pendulum to blaming others because we cannot seem to achieve lasting success, security, or control.

Once you find your ground again and begin to recover, tribulation is actually an opportunity, a starting place to heal your beliefs because nobody is going to do it for you, and nobody can heal you but you. This is boggling and requires uncommon conviction as well as deeper understanding.

Are you ready to dive into the beliefs that are no longer working for you? Possibly beliefs that you've based your whole life upon?

The pages before you will bank toward spiritual healing as opposed to psychological approaches. Psychology is primarily concerned with the mind: the way we think, formulate concepts, understand the world around us, and make sense of it. We'll be taking an otherworldly approach. Spirituality in a sense is an opening—an invitation, if you will—to go beyond the concepts of self, wants, and desires, bridging the way to transcendence. In a nutshell, psychology is about trying to "fix" your self-image, while spirituality is realizing that your concept of a self-image is actually an illusion.

Like me, you may feel as if you've been taken hostage by overwhelming emotions and thoughts that elicit remorse, anger, blame, and, worst of all, the paralyzing belief that the world is somehow against you, no matter how hard you've worked to improve your life. Plagued with low self-esteem, lack of confidence, and even feelings of unworthiness.

Perhaps there is a lifeline, a promise of safety and survival, that continues to drift just out of your reach. You are hopeless, helpless, and sort of in limbo not knowing how to achieve the childlike authenticity and happiness you were promised upon taking responsibility for your life by doing the inner work.

The right doors opened up for me once I became willing to ask for help, and if the words on the pages that poured through me let into you a crack of light, I consider my purpose in life achieved. For all I wish to provide is a bridge to accessing your teacher within.

You see, this book is really about healing myself—who am I, but you in truth, for we are all one. By processing fully and reconciling the horror that I think happened to me, I am healing you which is, indeed, reciprocal. For I have found that what appears to be going on inside is projected onto the people and the world seen on the outside.

The paradox of healing is realizing there is no healing needed, for you are already whole, and complete right here, right now. Hence, the belief that we need healing temporarily overshadows the truth of your perfect, pristine wholeness.

Though my original goal was to communicate love and light through this writing, it turns out it's more about uncovering the ploys of the ego and moving through the barriers to the realization that we are perfect peace by courageously diving into and through the very obstacles that we believe are robbing us of peace. The primary focus within the non-dualistic spiritual philosophy of *A Course in Miracles* instructs us on how to undo the lies of the ego. So, what you're actually healing is your beliefs to the contrary. Detaching and disengaging from all your misery, which is sourced from the small mind or ego. The untruths that dance about in your head.

You will encounter the terms "ego," the small self, the lower mind, and wrong-mindedness, all used interchangeably throughout this book, referring to the part of us that thinks it can be separate from the whole as if a wave can be apart from the ocean.

My goal is to inspire, for inspiration begets sound action. Inspired thought is found by navigating your way through the clouds that obscure the love and light within. The chatter, old beliefs, past pain, anxiety, chronic busyness, and health issues that color our lives are what make up these imaginary clouds that appear to block us. We are being asked to walk through these clouds by stepping out in trust and faith until we come out on the other side where our mutual brilliance is revealed. This is our purpose beyond worldly goals.

In the brief instant that it takes to come back to center, we regain our authenticity and find real peace, joy, love, and beauty once again.

Some say I gained my expertise through hard knocks due to the trauma and tragedy that riddled my childhood. Addiction, poverty, suicide, mental illness, and premature deaths plagued my family. This led me to learning and practicing meditation, the twelve steps of Al-Anon and Alcoholics Anonymous, and then to studying the concepts of *A Course in Miracles* since 1985. This later led me to speak and facilitate groups on spiritual philosophy based on love. bioSynergy Better Health, a holistic wellness practice, was founded as a result, followed by the creation of the Higher Self Care series—retreats, workshops, and private integrative wellness programs based on the 5 Steps to Higher Self Care.

Dear reader, if you have picked up this book or found it online, take it to the next level. Raise your capacity for enlightenment, authenticity, and peace by diving in with complete abandon. What you read may shock, bore, or inspire you. No matter, considering that the point is for you to move just one step closer toward healing the misperceptions that have kept you stuck and living small. Dive in and breathe into all that surfaces because the pain, memories, and self-doubt are precisely what is asking to be healed in you now. As the iconic author Louise Hay says, "The point of power is always in the present moment." What are you waiting for?

Part I: Crashing Waves

Chapter 1: Humble Beginnings

"This is the law the miracle obeys; that healing sees no specialness at all. It does not come from pity but from love. And love would prove all suffering is but a vain imagining, a foolish wish with no effects."

—*A Course in Miracles* (T-27.II.7:4-6)

Looking back, my childhood was much like a living expression of "The Great Wave off Kanagawa," the famous Hokusai print. The waves were too much, too much for a helpless child tossed like a cork in turbulent waters. Those waters, my father's violent outbursts, were wave after wave crashing down around me with no time for recovery, leaving me gasping for survival on the sheer ice-cold cliffs of my benumbed and despairing mother who could offer no respite. And upon me again, the next wave blindsiding me with my father's inner mental hell juxtaposed against a stark, cold, dark emptiness. There was nothing to hold onto, not even my mother. The combination was daunting.

Jack, my father, met Katie, my mother, when he was stationed on the East Coast in Wareham, Massachusetts. An unplanned pregnancy precipitated marriage just two days after mom's eighteenth birthday. They went on to raise five of us, me the eldest, in Northern California in what some might call extreme dysfunction.

Now married and a young mother, Katie was living three thousand miles from her family. She was likely haunted by her own childhood traumas, while Jack most certainly suffered through the inner hell of mental illness. I am sure that, steeped in the bliss of falling for each other, they believed their young love would make every wrong in their world right again.

Why do we have this idealistic belief that two people meet, fall in love, marry, make a home, have children, and live happily ever after? Boggling, isn't it, when this is rarely the case? Of course we lacked much in that fairy tale version, and I spent years feeling inadequate, certain there was something terribly wrong. An irrational response, as there were hints others hadn't figured it out either. When invited to a neighbor's or a classmate's home, I almost always picked up on a lurking air of secrecy and discord in spite of appearances.

I remember mom's moods often ranged from despondent and sort of vacant to cursing like a sailor in outbursts of anger with intermittent spurts of song, joking around, and laughter. She loved babies, but still it was no small chore with one baby after another. Imagine the toll on her body from having four pregnancies in succession, with the fifth child coming much later, and the years of feeding and bathing us—not to mention endless rinsing, washing, and line drying cloth diapers.

On the other hand, dad was only nineteen when they became parents and had recently been hospitalized for the first of three separate stays during the fifties and sixties for what was referred to as a nervous breakdown. It is often characterized by a period of severe depression or anxiety that suddenly becomes so overwhelming that a person can't function in their day-to-day life. Imagine the pressure of having to support a family with no college education, trained only as an airplane mechanic in the service. I remember him coming home exhausted and stressed and then taking it out on us. Like a hawk searching for prey he zeroed in on our every move. We had to eat with our mouths closed and not make a chomping sound lest we get slapped across the face, often getting knocked to the floor at the dinner table. After supper we were to sit quietly and perfectly still while we watched television as a family.

We were punished for crying. When I think about this now, the sound of a crying child does unnerve most of us. I wonder if it triggered within my father his own suppressed tears, causing him to stifle any whimpering at all costs. Oddly, laughter and giggling were just as quickly shut down as if it wasn't okay to have fun. *How dare you feel joy* was the message received.

On one occasion that I shall never forget, mom, presently caring for an infant, toddler, and two preschoolers, was desperate for a cigarette and didn't have a driver's license, which limited her mobility and sense of independence. She handed me a note and instructed me to carefully walk to the neighbor's house down our long driveway and up the neighbor's long driveway to deliver the message. I assume she didn't know the neighbor or her telephone number, or maybe we didn't have a phone at the time. She might as well have asked me to trek the Pacific Crest Trail and knock on the door of the Sasquatch. Nonetheless, I did as I was told.

When I arrived at the door, I handed the stranger the note mom had given me and asked to borrow a cigarette for my mommy. Regardless of the handwritten note there still seemed to be a lot of confusion, I eventually got the two or three cigarettes and walked down the long driveways back home.

In the meantime dad had come home from work and must have completely flipped out because as soon as I walked in the door he jerked me into the house and beat me with the belt to what felt like the edge of my life. Like a dazed bird that had slammed into a window, this was a horrendous shock. What had I done wrong? Horrified, all mom could do was stand by helplessly. There were many, many more times when I didn't know why I was beaten. None of us did. If we knew why or what we'd done wrong then maybe we could avoid the spankings. I use the term spanking loosely, as spanking is typically less severe than inflicting bruises or bodily harm. Witnessing my younger siblings being punished was worse—every cell in my body seemed to absorb the blows as their cries felt like needles puncturing my heart.

I recall as a four year old desperately yearning to go to school like the neighborhood children, partly in hopes of getting away from the unpredictable surroundings where every interaction seemed upside down and mixed up. When I did finally enter school, I quickly figured out that you got rewarded for correct answers and good grades and excelled despite moving every year or two to a new school. Because the boundaries were clearer, I discovered what was up and down, right and wrong, good and bad, black and white. These minute consistencies allowed me to flourish in school. It was discovered by Mrs. Crowe, my second-grade teacher that I could draw too.

Like other children who live in extreme dysfunction, I may have had an increased risk for a number of problematic developmental issues, including impaired cognition, which put me at a disadvantage. Consequently, I had to work harder to achieve good grades. Although wary of adults because of the chaos at home, I got good at reading my teachers by tapping into my sixth sense. This is how I got the praise that I longed for and the answer to needed adoration. Even our parents, especially dad, praised and rewarded us for good grades.

A trip to Nanny and Grandpa's house was our port in the storm because they were such loving and gentle, if not happy, drunks. I say this with all due respect for who they really were beyond the alcohol. Like most children we found our grandparent's home warm and welcoming. Every time I smell or even hear the sound of percolating coffee it brings me back to their kitchen. I still have in my possession the china set my father purchased for his mother, which he had shipped from Korea where he was stationed in the late 1950s. These dishes provided then, and still do, many bountiful holiday feasts. Once we were excused from a holiday meal we would rush over to our grandparents so they could feel how big our overstuffed bellies were while praising us for eating everything on our plates.

Nanny would cuddle us and stroke us lovingly with her elegantly painted fingernails. She cooked scrumptious fried chicken with green onion gravy and baked lemon meringue and banana cream pies. Grandpa possessed the kindest eyes and warmest smile. He seemed almost jovial at times and never raised his voice. He was a man who loved music and would play his favorites over and over again. I still remember my delight when listening to an old rendition of "Goodnight Irene" and "Mr. Lonely" by Bobby Vinton. I'm told my grandpa was a deliverer of door-to-door singing telegrams when he was a young man.

Occasionally we got to spend the night at their house, sometimes just one of us but usually two of us at a time. What a glorious reprieve as we were fed well and even a little spoiled the entire visit. No doubt they gave our parents money during their only son's hospitalizations and periods of unemployment. To this day I'll never know if our grandparents knew about the violence we endured at home. Though they thought highly of their gifted and intelligent only son, I'm certain they must have suspected his unsound, if not erratic, tendencies.

We had moved numerous times locally, probably due to rental leases not being renewed or eviction notices. When I was five we had moved in as many years. For what seemed like a long while, dad only came home on weekends; apparently, he committed himself to the mental health ward for a second time. There was always a lot of hush-hush surrounding these hospital stays. Years later it dawned on me that my father may have suffered from a severe mental illness, such as some form of paranoid schizophrenia, as I overheard Nanny say he used to hear voices, or perhaps something along the lines of intermittent explosive disorder, an often overlooked mental disorder that usually begins in childhood and is identified by sudden anger and episodes of impulsive, aggressive, violent behavior in which the person loses control entirely.

Like a puppy waiting for his long-absent master, I spent hours gazing out the window, hoping for daddy to come home. This time, to my delight, when he finally arrived back from the psychiatric hospital he had brought with him a friend who'd be staying with us until he got back on his feet. His name was Guy, and upon being introduced to him I walked into the middle of the living room and twirled my dress, after which I received a sound spanking. Between my sobs, I heard Guy mumble under his breath his objection to this act.

Falling to Pieces

I don't know what prompted the third longest and final hospital stay approximately five years later, but it lasted the better part of a year. All I knew was all the king's horses and all the king's men couldn't put daddy together again. During his final stay at the Veterans Administration psychiatric hospital he made another good friend, Mr. Lester Daniels. He had some property and invited dad to put a trailer on it and relocate the family to Chico, two and a half hours north of the Bay Area, which seemed like oceans away from Nanny and Grandpa. I was about ten by then, and our mother had just come home with their fifth child, our newborn baby brother, Martin.

It was in Chico that we were introduced to country living, with horses, livestock, chickens, dogs, and rabbits. Situated across the street from us was an almond orchard and a dairy farm where we could purchase milk with cream on top for fifty cents a gallon. Dad started raising black Labrador dogs to sell, but watching him mistreat and beat the dogs was too much for us kids to bear.

As youngsters we watched in awe as our mom magically produced tomato soup by adding water to a nearly empty ketchup bottle, shaking it well, and warming it up on the stovetop. Somehow in the preceding years they could afford school clothes for us in September, but it was around this time when we had to make do with hand-me-downs. As I grew into adolescence I would scrape and save my birthday money—my only source of income—so I could purchase clothes that looked more "in." I was so embarrassed by the free lunches that I would work for the school cafeteria to earn my meals. That way my classmates didn't know that our family was poor.

Dad had come from more comfortable means, but mom, the youngest of nine, was raised in poverty. Impoverished still, and in more ways than one, mom also suffered from debilitating depression. I absorbed mom's sadness and despair, which engulfed me. I just wanted to help, and honestly, every fiber of my being wanted to help dad too. Mom often confided in me, the sensitive eldest who seemed to have wisdom beyond her years and was a good listener even as a small child. She once told me that dad became green with jealousy, forbade her from any contact with her friends, and would shut her down quickly when she tried to make a new friend. Thinking back, I am pretty sure their peers, especially the women who wanted to befriend my mother, must have been aghast, if not suspicious, of dad's controlling behavior.

After less than a couple of years on Mr. Daniels' property, we moved our little forty-foot trailer, which now housed the seven of us, twenty minutes southeast to an isolated area near Oroville. With four acres surrounded by miles of rice fields, it remains a mystery how our father was able to swing the purchase of this property. Our only neighbor was an elderly ranching couple at least a mile away who kept to themselves.

We kids named our property "Lone Tree Ranch," for it had only a single tree as far as the eye could see. Now we were really cut off from outside contact, and to escalate matters during the seventies, Big Foot sightings were making the news, so we were on the lookout for Big Foot coming around when dad was away participating in horse shows or weekend archery and trapshooting competitions.

Not long after our move, our beloved Nanny was diagnosed with emphysema and stayed with us on the four acres briefly before she passed away. Nanny and mom were great friends and she took Nanny's passing hard, as did dad. What a blessing to have a mother-in-law that you adore. Maybe aggravated by the heartache of losing a dear friend, it seemed mom's frailty and depression had noticeably worsened as if a balloon deflated inside and part of her simply gave up.

We were unable to afford groceries and applied for welfare aid from the state. We received commodities monthly: blocks of cheese, dried beans, flour, oatmeal with bugs in it, sugar, cornmeal, powdered milk, powdered eggs, and other various staples. For most of those years even a piece of fruit was a rare delicacy. Mom was thankful for the welfare, but from my perspective it seemed dad's pride took a hit.

Billy, the second eldest, and I would hike and explore for miles outside the perimeter of the property whenever we could. One time Billy split open his inner thigh on a barbed wire fence and mom, who'd recently gotten her driver's license, almost fainted before she got him to a hospital for stitches. A week before we had been hopping fences and came across a bull. As I rambled along Billy shouted, "Get to the other side quick!" I had been oblivious to the snorting, annoyed beast pawing the earth and preparing to charge. Another amazing sight was a snake that stretched across the entire dirt road in front of our house. Snakes were common in Northern California, and while most were harmless, they were big.

Billy and I would run through the fields for a long, long way. He was so athletic, and I wanted to be like him even though he was my little brother. On one occasion, though, no matter how hard I tried to keep up, I struggled to breathe. When we got back to the house I collapsed onto the daybed in the living room, panicking, wheezing, and scared to death. Mom took me to the doctor, which was not what usually happened with an illness, but I think we were receiving Medicaid at the time.

All through my childhood if one of us got sick, and I always seemed to be sick, mostly with ear aches or the flu, my mother applied cold washcloths to the forehead and fed us aspirin and milk toast. In other words, if we got sick we just didn't go to the doctor. I don't think I was given antibiotics until I was a twenty-year-old, which made me sicker than a dog. Even now I wonder if, by staying out of the doctor's office combined with not having access to processed convenience and fast foods, we were actually healthier because we demanded more from our immune systems.

The day after the severe wheezing incident, though, I was taken to the doctor. The doctor came in after some tests with his prognosis of exercise-induced asthma complicated by mononucleosis. I was laid up for six weeks in bed, doing my best to keep my grades up at home. As a budding eighth grader I might as well have been shackled in an isolated dungeon in medieval times. Soon after I had another bout of tonsillitis, so they decided to have my tonsils removed. My asthma worsened after the surgery. As a matter of fact, everything worsened, with hay fever that became almost debilitating, and both maladies plagued me until, in my thirties, I discovered holistic health and a world of alternatives to surgery and pharmaceuticals.

On the four acres of Lone Tree Ranch we raised chickens, pheasants, quail, pigeons, and rabbits, pastured two horses, and grew a huge garden, which included tomatoes, corn, and watermelon. Now we were eating well. Amidst our cornucopia of plenty, we kids feasted on garden delights to our hearts' content and used to have contests to see who could eat the most corn on the cob or watermelon. Mom couldn't get enough of the luscious garden-fresh tomatoes and would make tomato and mayonnaise sandwiches.

Kindling

We were already impoverished and isolated when a fire erupted in our tiny domicile. It was such a small trailer, more reminiscent of a camper really. I was in the top bunk, and my two younger brothers shared the bottom bunk below, which was nestled in the hallway so narrow you could barely walk through. My sisters shared a cot basically at the back end of the trailer. The upside of owning our own trailer meant nobody could evict us. It didn't help that my mother was constantly cleaning, which was probably therapeutic given the circumstances. The cleaning included regularly polishing the wood paneling throughout our home. This caustic wood polish was no doubt combustible, providing the perfect kindling like gasoline on a campfire.

Was the volatility in our home enough to spark the fire? I wonder. Could the property be under some curse? Folks said there were two other homes on this property lost to fire previous to ours. On February 4, 1972, just before my thirteenth birthday, Pamela woke up and told mom that she smelled smoke. Dad rushed us outside, and in a flash the whole house was aflame. He'd hollered at Billy to bring the hose around to the front, but by the time he handed the spewing nozzle to him the rubber hose had melted in half.

With the blind courage of a lioness protecting her young, mom bolted back into the trailer to retrieve two-year-old Martin, who was forgotten inside in the confusion. Dad went back in to get valuables but singed his eyebrows in the process. There was nothing left to do. We loaded into the car, pulled out on the lonesome dirt road, and watched in disbelief as our home went up in smoke. Boom! Bang, pop, boom! Bang, crack, pop! We were suddenly jolted when dad's collection of guns and ammunition ignited in the blaze, and for fifteen straight minutes it sounded like World War II was upon us. Thank goodness little sister Pamela smelled the smoke in our home and bravely woke mom and dad, saving all of our lives.

With nothing left we were reduced to wearing out-of-date clothing from the thrift store. Some items were too big or too small. I felt so humiliated at school, no longer able to hide our economic status. I shall never forget the putrid smell during the weeks of foraging through the ashes of metal structure, melted appliances, rubber, wood, and clothing, reduced to charcoal now soaked with water from the high-pressured fire hoses in hopes of finding any valuables that may have survived, such as dad's extensive coin collection, mom's wedding ring, or anything else that could be salvaged. Dad said, "I didn't know pennies could melt" when Jackie discovered his coin collection under the ashes some distance from where they were stored, carried by the act of combustion, I suppose.

With the birthday card money I'd received in the mail a week before the fire, I'd bought a pair of sandals and white jeans, which were all the rage at the time. At last I could fit in with the popular girls at school. Regrettably, as I made my way out of the burning trailer, dazed from coming out of a sound sleep with my covers over my nose and mouth, an unconscious act to filter out the suffocating fumes, I pushed the new outfit back onto the bed along with my clarinet. None of those items survived the fire that destroyed our home. I realize today that because the top bunk was the highest point of the small trailer, I was in very real danger of smoke inhalation.

Eventually after a few months of staying with Great Aunt Lethie, Nanny's eldest sister, and Uncle Curt, who resided a couple towns south of us, the trailer was replaced with a bigger one by an insurance settlement, no doubt. Just before I was to enter my freshman year of high school and not much more than a year after the fire, our family moved again, this time out of state, to a location where we were no longer isolated. To our relief we had neighbors in the trailer park. This gave the eldest of us the opportunity to earn money babysitting, washing dishes at the local truck stop, and doing other odd jobs.

With skyrocketing unemployment in California, Aunt Leoda, Nanny's older sister, and Uncle Jerry Dale, who ran a small construction company, guaranteed dad work as a finish carpenter in Colorado, where the Vail ski area was booming with new construction. You might say our lives had finally taken a turn for the better in just about every way.

Chapter 2: Strange Dreams

"Learn that even the darkest nightmare that disturbs the mind of God's sleeping Son holds no power over him. He will learn the lesson of awaking. God watches over him and light surrounds him."

—*A Course in Miracles* (T-13.XI.9:5-7)

Adolescence isn't easy for any parent to navigate. We kids were doing what teenagers do, trying to become adults, gain our independence, and grow up. Sassiness, not picking up after ourselves, and pushing any limits we could was, well, just part of the process. Mom took the brunt of this because we dared not disobey dad ever.

The water gave us giardia, and most of us were quite ill for the first two weeks after arriving in Colorado. Once we recovered, things seemed more stable with our brand-new even-bigger mobile home, having neighbor kids our ages nearby, and dad securing gainful employment. Yet the volatility in our household continued. To complicate matters, dad's need to control us was heightened by the many new outside influences. During this period, we were not allowed to join extra-curricular activities after school, attend sports events, or stay up past nine p.m. Though it appeared he'd loosened the reins a bit when the youngest of us three girls, Pamela, entered high school, as she was given permission to play sports. Was it because she dared to ask, or had dad lightened up?

The need for control, as I understand it, stems from fear, and in my mind that was my dad's true affliction—fear, masquerading as paranoid violent outbursts and mental instability. From my perspective, the medications only dulled his awareness and connection to himself, so he was unable to "see" any way out of his personal anguish. That being said, maybe he really did not have within him the capacity as he would have lapses of memory after a violent episode, flummoxing his victims. Sometimes he talked to us sweetly, seemingly calm and composed afterward as if nothing had happened.

Our father was an amazing man beyond his mental illness. He had a tender and even nurturing side, speaking to us lovingly when we were sick. He taught me how to knit and he painted my nails for the first time when I was twelve. He knew exactly what to do in a crisis; where mom tended to panic, dad did not. Once while we were living on the four acres, I'd just set on the arm of his chair a scalding hot cup of tea he had asked me to make for him. Jackie scurried by, and, as he often grabbed us to tickle us as we walked by, he reached to grab her leg. The cup was knocked over, and the scalding liquid poured over her leg. As she cried out in agony, dad instinctively ripped off her pajamas and probably reduced the severity of the burns. She was still rushed to the hospital with second and third-degree burns over almost thirty percent of her body. To this day I shudder to think that it was my act that caused her such searing pain that would scar her for life. If only I hadn't set the tea down on the arm of the chair.

We quickly made new friends in our new school, and Billy and I both had a steady girlfriend and boyfriend. We were growing into adolescence. It was instant popularity as new students from California in this small mountain town in Colorado. In their eyes we were "cool" simply because we were from California. Meanwhile, to our astonishment many of the kids wore cowboy hats and boots, listened to country music, and introduced us to chewing tobacco, which luckily made us sick so we had good reason to opt out. These outdated, backward ways were viewed by us as nothing short of aliens from another planet. Nevertheless we lapped up the admiration and fast friendships.

Mom got a part-time job cleaning rooms at the local motel and finally began earning her own money. One of the highlights of her life was to drive to the town hall once a month to play Bingo, which, for some reason, dad allowed. One night she came home overjoyed. I'd never seen her so happy, grinning from ear to ear and bursting with pride and excitement with a one-hundred-dollar check in her hand.

Unfortunately, her elation was short lived. In the wake of a particularly rough spell, mom began ritualistically stopping by the liquor store in the early afternoon on her way home from work to secretly imbibe an entire six-pack before dad got home, thereby destroying the evidence. I'm sure this seemed to help her get through another day of not knowing when dad would fly into a rage, not to mention coping with two teens, two preteens, and a five-year-old.

We kids had money, too, doing odd jobs, babysitting, and washing dishes at Bernice's Restaurant and Bar. We would walk the couple of miles to Stanley's grocery store and purchase candy, twinkies, and sodas, which we didn't get at home, and proceed to binge eat them on the stroll back home. I suspect each of us found ways to diffuse the assiduousness of our circumstances.

As I write this, too many memories of the insanity we endured flood into my mind. I cannot write them down fast enough. Though it might be therapeutic, it serves no useful purpose to burden you, the reader, with them, for this book is about transcending hard times and not an account of the untold barbaric injustices that occur on this earth.

Do we really need a detailed rendering of trials to gain the miracle of peace, security, and love, no matter what a person goes through? That being said, there are at least two incidences I'm being called to record here, and as painful as it seems, I shall do so.

Fighting Back

As was the norm after supper at about seven p.m., we children took our seats on the couch to watch television with mom and dad, though mom preferred to read while we watched educational programs or whatever dad wanted that night. On this particular evening we'd just sat down to watch television when dad snapped at mom for not joining us. Sometimes he insisted that she watch television with us. On this occasion, however, the six beers she'd downed that afternoon had dulled the senses and lowered her instinct for safety as she replied, "Go to hell." This did not go over well, as you can imagine. My father in that instant appeared to me as a big cat ready to pounce. In reaction to her sharp retort, he sprang out of his recliner and jerked her by the heel of her right foot so hard that her book went flying. She shot out of her mustard-colored cushioned chair and landed flat on her back on the shag carpeting with a deafening thud.

A moment before she had been escaping into a romantic Western novel, her all-time favorite genre, wearing a purple and cream-colored horizontally striped sweater. I remember this like it was yesterday.

Immediately dad ordered all of us to march straight to bed, wielding blows as we frantically rushed past him. All of my siblings darted as fast as they could to our bedrooms. All of us except me. And like the straw that broke the camel's back, something inside of me screamed "No," and as I started toward the back of the house, that "No" became audible. I stood on the step leading into the kitchen, which made me appear taller than my father, and with hands on hips I shouted, "NO!" As he charged toward me, pointing his finger, he repeated, "Get to bed, now!" but stopped dead because, like an immovable boulder, I didn't budge and stared straight into his crazed green eyes.

Startled for a split second, dad froze and looked away, as if scanning his mind for direction. In that dire instant that he looked away, doubt overcame me, or you might say my sanity returned, or I second-guessed myself as something in my head said, *now what?* In that nanosecond his rage regained its potency. Wham! He threw me to the floor and dragged me by my hair like a rag doll, knocking me up against the walls of the long, narrow hallway as I struggled to free myself. He stood me up and pinned me by the throat against the dresser in the bedroom that I shared with my two younger sisters, Jackie and Pamela, who were already huddled in their beds in terror. It didn't occur to me that my life was in the balance, and oddly there was no sensation of the blows or missing clumps of hair.

My focus drifted behind my father's right shoulder, astonished, as I watched a chair being lifted up over his head. Apparently my mother decided to fight back, too, because by some otherworldly power she'd managed to lift a chair above her head with every intention of bringing it down upon him. And in what seemed almost choreographed in slow motion, like a move in Aikido, he pivoted in a single motion and with his right arm brushed her to the floor, redirecting her attack while simultaneously releasing his grip around my throat.

There was my brave mother lying on the floor, one fist still clenching the chair. Where did this frail woman muster that kind of strength? She may have saved my life. Was my father capable of killing me? Thankfully, we shall never know.

My sisters and I cried ourselves to sleep that night. Wracked with convulsive sobs, I prayed that what took place that evening was really just a horrible nightmare. Awakening the next day felt like coming out of a coma as I registered that this was no dream. I have no recollection of the pain during the assault, but I do remember the raw emptiness and despair of the next day, like a snapshot forever captured in my brain. Even more incredible is that my mother never uttered a word about this incident. I suppose it was neatly tucked away in a secluded corner of her psyche with the rest of the madness.

After one of these episodes the four eldest of us began regularly plotting my father's death in colorful detail. It scares me now to think of how we may have been capable of executing our well-thought-out plan. Perhaps our scheming kept us sane in the grips of these insane circumstances. I am certain, like soldiers in the midst of war, without the comradery I had with my siblings I would have long perished or certainly lost my mind.

My best friend at school insisted that I place a phone call to Sherriff Sebrey to inform him we were being beaten. Karen practically forced me to call. Sweating and shaking as I dialed the number, I poured out the story over the phone. He assured me that it wasn't as bad as I thought and there was nothing he could do. Once in a while someone would tip off social services and we'd get a home visit, but this only exasperated the dysfunction at home.

Survival required that I learn to take leave of my senses, and sometimes my dreams seemed more real than my waking circumstances at home. I've been told by more than one therapist that this is a survival technique known as dissociation.

Dissociation is a mental process where a person disconnects from their thoughts, feelings, memories, or sense of identity. In my case my eyes will look away in the distance, trancelike, and go blank.

I had a sixth sense. Not only was I "high strung," my Nanny's words for ultra-sensitive, but I seemed to know things my parents couldn't explain. As a preteen I began having dreams that would give me an answer or some direction. Then I started having clairvoyant visions of accidents that would happen soon after. This frightened me. Upon reaching adolescence, desperate to make sense of things and find my own answers, I began reading the Bible. I believed the devil had possessed me and deducted I was inherently evil. A part of me felt that I was deserving of punishment because somehow I was causing the accidents. I began praying for these prophetic phantoms to go away, and when I'd prayed hard enough, they did.

It wasn't until many years later that I would see this as a gift, and my heightened perception gradually returned mostly in waking visions, dreams, or as an uncanny inner knowing.

Just a Nightmare?

"Whatever suffers is not part of me. What grieves is not myself. What is in pain is but illusion in my mind. What dies was never living in reality, and did but mock the truth about myself."

—*A Course in Miracles* (W-248.1:3-6)

Speaking of dreams, I heard Billy calling me. It was really his voice, and I missed him so badly it hurt. Billy had opted out, shooting himself to death a few weeks before on the day that his young girlfriend had broken up with him. I know it wasn't the break-up that gave his young heart no alternative. Rather, it was reflective of the culmination of years of abuse with no way out, as he had tried to run away a month before, only to be located after three days and returned home.

Billy was just fourteen, and it would've been the summer before he entered high school. For weeks after this unspeakable loss we kids and our parents each struggled in our own ways, sometimes forgetting our names, how to breathe or walk, unable to distinguish the days from the nights. Our eyes and faces were swollen from the inability to cease sobbing while numb to the rest of the world. In the high school yearbook that came out a couple of weeks after, a teacher who'd known him, I'm still not sure who it was, had the foresight to put a full-page photo with a poem that couldn't have been more perfect for Billy and his sudden exit, commemorating his brief trek on this earth. I am writing this book for Billy. I saw him as a friend who could never be replaced. Perhaps you have known someone as dear.

"There Are Some Men"

There are some men
who should have mountains
to bear their names to time.

Grave-markers are not high enough
or green,
and sons go far away
to lose the fist
their father's hand will always seem.

I had a friend:
he lived and died in mighty silence
and with dignity,
left no book, son, or lover to mourn.

Nor is this a mourning-song
but only a naming of this mountain
on which I walk,
fragrant, dark, and softly white
under the pale of mist.
I name this mountain after him.

—Leonard Cohen

As I was saying, in the most vivid dream I heard Billy's voice calling my name—Donna, Donna, Donna—beckoning me to go with him. I was holding hands with the other young teenagers who lived in the neighborhood. We'd formed a large circle in the horse pasture that led to Hockett Gulch and the mountains we explored like ants on an anthill.

Billy continued to call, and I decided I would go with him, breaking the chain of maybe ten other teens. I let go of Cindy's hand on my left, but she stood in front of me and pleaded, "Don't go." I still had Susan's hand in my right and was ready to let go of her hand, too, for every fiber of my being was committed to following Billy once again. I wanted to see my brother so very badly, and the source of his voice was coming from those mountains. If I let go of Susan's hand it was all over. After a grueling inner tug of war, I overcame the urge to break free of the circle and follow Billy one last time. With complete resolution I re-clasped Cindy's hand. I shuddered when I awoke, believing fully that if I had broken free of the interlocked circle and followed the voice I might not be here. I fully believed that I would have crossed over.

In my fifteen-year-old head I believed that so completely, and who is to know if following Billy's voice would have moved me into another realm? On some level, it became apparent to me, even though I didn't want to ignore him. I'd no choice but to resist his call and stay here a while longer.

I have no clue why recording these incidents was necessary. Perhaps it was meant for you to hear, not to dwell on the pain and suffering we've all endured but to instead turn our focus to the peace that links us. The peace which passeth all understanding. Pain and suffering are universal—par for the course in this egoic world, and, in my mind, relative. Pain is pain, loss is loss, trauma is trauma, no matter the specifics.

Chapter 3: Tossed Like a Cork

"God did not create a meaningless world . . . is another step in learning to let go the thoughts that you have written on the world. . . . Some of them will lead you directly into fear. You will not be left there. You will go far beyond it. Our direction is toward perfect safety and perfect peace.

—*A Course in Miracles* (W-14.1:1–3:6)

Due to the exposure to such chaos in my childhood, my social skills may have been somewhat arrested and developed strangely. Not only was I as timid as a fawn, but I gravitated toward bullies and allowed myself to be pushed around. For example, in second grade I followed after Sandra, a classmate who towered over me. I trailed behind her like a lost puppy dog during recess when she would frequently stop in her tracks to holler at me and slap me across the face. Bringing my hand to my stinging cheek I would vow to obey her. This peculiar pattern, though less severe, continued into high school as my best friend, Karen, whom I deemed perfect in every way, blonde, slender, confident, and beautiful, became like a god to me. I wanted to be as popular as her, so I mimicked her to the extreme by doing whatever she wanted. I talked like her, dressed like her, cut classes, and even stole earrings on one occasion, much of what was truly against what I believed to be right and wrong just to win her approval.

The dark repercussions caused by fear-based acts are more widespread than we can imagine. It would seem that Sandra endured ill treatment, too, for her attacks were not those of an innocent child. She was only acting out what she was most likely experiencing at home. Her irrational conduct seemed more normal for me than playing amiably with others, so I continued to follow her around at recess into the third grade before we moved yet again. As for Karen, it appeared that she had a normal family. Is that really possible, though? Her patterns were internal, such as a gnawing ego-driven insecurity that compelled her to dominate in order to feel safe and valued, perhaps with the belief that she wasn't okay unless she was in control. I suppose, like me, these schoolmates were just trying to compensate for their insecurities in the only way that they knew how.

This inability to assert myself carried over into boys too. I would agree to date a boy just because he asked, never really knowing if I liked him or not. Ideally, teenagers are better prepared— being educated about sex and given the guidance to help them understand the reality and potential gravity of their actions. They are more empowered to know when to say no instead of following blindly without the resources to make a mindful choice. And yes, as a teen, sometimes without influence from peers, I would deliberately choose the rebellious acts too.

The tumultuous circumstances during my upbringing may have stunted my ability to know myself, which was more serious than a mere identity crisis. What I wanted and what was safe for me were unknown. Children will know how to become responsible adults when you teach them by example, bestowing the ability to make sound decisions and, most importantly, to be responsible to themselves. You cannot be there all the time to guide them. Ideally, you teach them to know and trust themselves. Testing their curiosity, they'll choose paths that may seem inimical now and then, hopefully, without irreversible consequences. And that's precisely how they learn to make better choices in the future. That is also how Spirit guides us gently toward the choices that bring us peace.

I did not have that stable and nurturing guidance. Instead, when very young, I formed the mistaken idea that love equated to "getting attention," and that included the backward notion that any attention meant love. Allowing myself to be pushed around because of thwarted modeling was just part of the roles I took on due to my early life experiences. A butterfly sometimes needs the tight, closed-in struggle of the cocoon in order to build the strength to fly.

In their delusion my parents were simply unable to provide that foundation. Consequently, as teens, Jackie and Pamela acted out experimenting with marijuana, and in my case, it was boys. All I knew was to give what I thought another wanted. I just wanted to help, so I helped others at my expense, not ever really knowing who Donna was in the confusion. The irony is that the self we're looking for, once we think we've found it, isn't really who we are, for as we grow toward the light we discover our oneness with all—our true identity.

This was, of course, the construct to sleep with the first boy who gave me attention, and soon I found myself pregnant and married at the tender age of sixteen.

If I were to judge my parents, I would surely judge myself. This rigid attitude leaves no room for grace. If I couldn't forgive my parents, how could I forgive myself? As a teenage mom I was basically alone. Though my young husband, Kelley, and I had an official ceremony at the justice of the peace, he was apparently just as traumatized as I was. His way of trying to calm the horror within took the form of workaholism and drinking to excess, which meant parenting on my own a great deal of the time. We were so young and so unequipped to raise our two children, our first Jeremy and then Jacinda, born almost three years later. To make matters more unforgivably alarming, the cellular pent-up trauma that I'd absorbed into my very cells over the years began bubbling up in violent episodes mostly directed toward my son, a toddler.

An eighteen-year-old time bomb. As much as I vowed never to repeat the ill treatment that I had endured, it happened. Somehow I absorbed my father's violent behaviors, which erupted onto my son as his baby sister witnessed. Now the perpetrator, I was steeped in deep shame and feelings of guilt. These are the most painful emotions a soul endures in my mind.

Unable to set and stick to reasonable limits, I had no clue about how to discipline a child. I read to them, bathed and fed them, and tucked them into bed, but beyond that I just let them do what they wanted because I had never been modeled appropriate discipline methods. Anger would build up, which terrified me in the absence of the skills to discipline with love, meaning any upset was quickly repressed. I was ignorant of anything except severe punishment, and in my right mind that was the last thing I wanted my children to experience.

To my horror, my childhood trauma sparked abusive tendencies complicated by all the anger that I'd been trying to push away by escaping into compulsive, disordered eating at the time. These cyclical tendencies may be linked to an unconscious attempt to try and heal from past trauma or to regain a sense of control. Though it is hard to understand why someone who has been abused in childhood would engage in violence of any kind again, it occurs in some who've experienced harsh treatment. This pattern is known as the cycle of abuse.

"Let us today be neither arrogant nor falsely humble. We have gone beyond such foolishness. We cannot judge ourselves, nor need we do so."

—*A Course in Miracles* (W-154.1:1-3)

Does it serve us to punish ourselves? Isn't life already laced with unnecessary pain and anguish? We cling to self-hate for mistakes made in the past. However, as you'll find in the coming pages, grace is achieved only by honestly recognizing the mistakes and, with all the humility you can muster, asking for direction in that moment.

It's natural and even healthy to feel badly, guilty, or confused. However, the act of punishing yourself with periods of wallowing in guilt or depriving yourself of love and joy is just another mistake. Once you catch yourself, correction can begin.

Feelings of unworthiness do not imply that you are bad. It is just a reminder that you've gone off the path to peace, which is easy to do when taking ego suggestions. Lower emotions are an indication that you've chosen wrongly. The solution is simply to realize that with grace as you give up any guilt and ask for direction from your Higher Self. You experimented with the ego's direction, so now you can choose to listen to grace instead.

Still, I have allowed compassion to flow through me toward my caretakers. I cannot blame my parents' inability to choose differently, nor would blame serve any beneficial purpose. They were only following doctors' orders using the readily available resources at the time—prescription medications, cigarettes, and beer. These had massive side effects that kept them in their deluded fog and offered nothing to educate them on resolving the core issues, thus bypassing the necessary clarity for inner healing. I am blessed to have before me solutions to such problems.

In spite of the chaotic circumstances, I received so much love and goodness from both of my parents. Mom provided buckets of joy, love, song, a thirst for reading, laughter, and devotion. She was dedicated to family and passing on what her mother, whom she revered, had taught her, including homemaking and holiday rituals that had been passed down for generations. Dad gave me the love of the outdoors and the belief that I was a capable, intelligent being. He provided warmth and the art of mastery and exhibited creative innovation that I truly admired.

When I asked Jeremy about how he had experienced me in those days he gently told me and asked me not to feel badly. He mentioned how this unbalanced behavior taught him to become acutely aware of potential volatility and gave him the wherewithal to walk away from it whenever possible. Jeremy reports that he experienced me as caring but filled with fear. He could sense the ticking time bomb within his mother, ready to go off at any moment. Although he knew on some level that I cared very much for him despite my violent temper, my precious son hid in his room crying all too often.

I could not forgive myself for this uncontrollable madness and kept it locked away in shame for far too long. As you've probably gathered, hiding our mistakes and blaming ourselves only leads to more mistakes. The path of self-growth is lined with mistakes. Jeremy was right in describing the tension within me as a ticking time bomb, for something would snap inside me as a brittle tree branch breaks catastrophically when bearing the weight of strong winds—in my case suppressed emotion and the heavy snow of guilt that had me lashing out at my child.

The intent to punish myself so as to stave off guilt didn't make me better. It just perpetuated this cycle as I became more isolated until, thankfully, I could take no more and mentioned my outbursts to my therapist. With that, the out-of-control episodes subsided. The act of admitting my startling loss of composure to another freed me to begin to heal all that was pent up inside of me. And so began the long, sinuous journey of recovery. From that time forward, no matter the labyrinthine detours, I was dedicated to wellness, to life, to love. Somewhere deep inside I knew that even in the midst of disordered eating, eventual alcohol and substance abuse, control addiction, and codependency, there was a glimmer of hope. A hope that there must be a better way and that God did not create a meaningless world filled with pain and misery.

Chapter 4: The Robbers Too

"If only attack produces fear, and if you see attack as the call for help that it is, the unreality of fear must dawn on you. For fear *is* a call for love, in unconscious recognition of what has been denied."

—*A Course in Miracles* (T-12.I.8:12-13)

While sitting on mommy's lap, she asked me, "Who do you love?" I responded gleefully with all the innocence of a four-year-old, "I love everybody in the whole wide world, even the robbers and bad guys!" She laughed and repeated back to me, "Even the robbers?"

Many of us have gone through situations or heard accounts that convince us there are, in fact, evil people. A question I often get in my work is, "Aren't some people devoid of goodness?" They often back up their claim with, "Look at Hitler." The fact is people are either exhibiting love or fear. The latter appears to justify or rationalize controlling types of behaviors. Incidentally, filling the heads of your followers with fear is an excellent way to gain control of the masses. Unchecked fear consequently triggers antisocial behaviors, such as doing anything to get control, hence our prime example of Hitler. Those who take wrong-minded actions are still part of the whole who have allowed repressed fear to sever them from the love that would heal them.

During times of perceived attack and imagined abuse I have had a hard time hating and seeing anyone as intrinsically bad. Even after my father seemed to hurt me, he was looked upon with the reverent eyes of a child. Though I'd spent many years ruminating on the shocking behaviors of others, some ancient memory reminded me that beyond this world each one of us is by nature pure and good.

Yet I've been plenty bewildered by the actions of others, including my own. Do my actions make me bad? Do my mistakes condemn me to hell? Do yours? Am I evil? Are you? Are we capable of anything but love? Does believing we are bad or they are bad help us to heal in any way? When a coach encourages you, you excel, and when he ridicules you, you do worse. If we withhold love, we only add to the illusion of separation.

As a child in elementary school, I used to become jittery when I walked home from school or around the neighborhood, certain that the "devil" was chasing me. And as I grew into adulthood, I had a foreboding that there were negative energies out to sabotage me, causing me to become obsessed with an inner warning that something bad was going to happen at any moment. It wasn't uncommon that a period of happiness would immediately be doused by a fitful night's sleep, illness, or the spiral of addictive behaviors as if it wasn't okay to be joyful.

Decades later I finally made peace with this nagging terror—the conviction that Satan stalked my every move. After years of diving head-first into meditation, which roused me to study various spiritual philosophies, including *A Course in Miracles*, I've come to some definitive insights. Everything is projected energy, and everything we experience is but a reflection of our beliefs about ourselves. What we see, sense, and feel reflects unprocessed emotion resulting from low-minded thoughts run amok.

In my experience, fearful encounters stem from unprocessed emotion. In other words, if you suppress low-frequency emotions—such as shame, fear, or anger—it shows up in your life. The great news is that this offers you another opportunity to let go of this lingering emotional residue for good. When you take a look inside and acknowledge the emotion, be fully present with it and give it space to be there for at least ninety seconds. That's all it takes to dissolve it.

As you practice dissolving lower-frequency emotions in this way, watch your life become lighter, freer, and more joyful. We'll dive deeper into the simplicity of this process as well as offer genuine examples as we journey through Part III.

Emotions are not tangible and are, essentially, just energy flowing through as water courses through an aqueduct. They are not reflective of who we are. You are not your emotions, and it's safe to welcome that uncomfortable feeling so that it doesn't appear in your outer world in the form of so-called "evil spirits." In my mind there are no evil spirits, devils, or possessed beings apart from our wayward imaginations.

For instance, a psychic client, Carla, was very in tune with energy patterns in the unseen world and convinced there was a demonic entity occupying her bedroom closet. She could feel it. It was her belief, so I honored her experience, not denying it, knowing that I, too, had experienced my own bouts of heightened awareness. As we progressed in her holistic wellness sessions it was revealed she had a great deal of unfounded guilt and hidden fears. I supported her to healthfully process and walk through the dark emotions until she was able to release the residues of apprehension and remorse. Weeks into the program the entities disappeared without a trace. My theory: Releasing the repressed emotion was all that was needed, for she was projecting the guilt into the ethers. When she identified, acknowledged, and let go of these strong, low-frequency feelings, the entity that seemed so very real to Carla disappeared from the closet too.

"The ultimate purpose of projection is always to get rid of guilt."

—*A Course in Miracles* (T-13.II.1:1)

You are good to your core—no matter what you believe you have or haven't done. We live in a world of goodness spackled with a lot of unprocessed fear controlling people's actions. From a higher perspective, our seemingly unkind acts, even my father's, stem from fear of separation and the belief that we can be rejected and apart from love.

The ego pendulates. We are better than or less than. We are right or wrong. It keeps us separate and alone. We are sure that we have been unfairly treated, so we languish in victimhood or try to control, doing our best to dominate others. Now we're playing the role of the perpetrator, unwittingly reinforcing the cycle of fear, anger, and shame that leads us to hang our heads again in disgrace. Nonetheless it only takes a shift in focus to realize you and I are equal, perfectly innocent, and whole. This dissolves the cloud of fear into timeless peace and tranquility.

It is sheer fantasy to see ourselves as victims—either helpless, hopeless and unworthy, inferior and imperfect or, conversely, superior, wiser, more beautiful, arrogant, and all-knowing—for we are, in truth, a note in one precious song that continues to call. It is incomplete while we dream of separation because you are a part of God's mind. Our better-than or worse-than delusional evaluations of ourselves and others are erroneous. You are very holy. Everyone is good simply because they exist.

Take your magnifying glass out. I ask you to consider the person who committed an unforgivable act and look at him or her. Look at them more closely into the tiny molecules and the atoms of the energy field that shapes their bodily form. Raise your vibration by focusing in on that person in your mind's eye until you find a light in them, even if it's a tiny glimmer. Your higher vision was created to find the light in others. When you find that spark in another, it activates a chain reaction that expands to encompass them and is simultaneously given to you. This light is love, the love that you are, the love that they are, and the love that I am. As a wave is to the sea, we are one in light.

Please bear in mind that as soon as you fall asleep again in the egoic nightmare, away from this holy instant, the small, negative mind chatter will once again take over. In any event, you can be certain that you've made headway.

When we focus on form and our ego's way of manipulating a mistake into a sin, it's almost impossible to see beyond it. The stories of the small mind are geared to hide the light, keeping the cycle of doom and gloom chugging along full steam ahead. Be willing to detach. Ask Spirit to pierce through the fog for an instant and connect with the love that makes us one. The Universe—one song of love. It only takes a nanosecond of willingness to shift your focus.

To illustrate, I flew to Kona, Hawaii, to attend a Sedona Method retreat many years ago. One participant, Barbara, a mature, handsome woman who was sharp as a whip and a strong personality, disrupted the flow of the lessons. Through the week-long seminar with a torrent of snappy criticism, she repeatedly challenged the expertise of the instructors and voiced blatant disgust at the, "in her opinion," mediocre content being presented. The small group, including the instructors, did a good job of overlooking this barrage of negativity. It seemed there was something wrong with just about everything, even the accommodations. I avoided her as best I could for most of the week.

In a casual format, the seminar participants were in a discussion led by the co-instructor. Barbara had the floor and spoke for a while, and while listening, my resistance toward her seemed to only magnify her faults. I asked God, *Help me to see her differently*, because at this point I was really struggling with my "unconditionally love everyone" spiritual commitment. With that I became aware of a soft voice as my inner teacher reminded me of one *A Course in Miracles* lesson that entails looking for light in another, especially someone who annoys you. I then became willing to see her differently.

As the lesson directs, it began with looking for a tiny glimmer of light in the person. Why not? It can't hurt to try. Thereby I narrowed my focus, intent on finding some beauty in her while she spoke. At last I detected it, so dim at first, yet there it was in her left eye. As it grew I realized this soft, distant glow like a shining star on a cold winter night had appeared in both of her eyes. Had it been there all along? It grew brighter and more beautiful, expanding into her heart. In that holy instant I was overcome with a warm feeling toward her. Then it seemed to expand brightly into her limbs, and, as if it had nowhere to go, it encompassed her body and expanded into me. Before this experiment felt complete, she abruptly stopped her monologue in mid-sentence and looked at me from across the room, straight into my eyes, and said, "Do you know how beautiful you are?" Stunned for a moment, I had confirmation of the miracle of looking for love where darkness seemed to prevail. The darkness of judgment that had blinded me.

I often reflect on this well-known late-nineteenth-century debate with a student and his professor. Whether it's true or not, it makes perfect sense in my mind and supports my theory above.

> "You measure the amount of light present. Isn't this correct? Darkness is a term used by man to describe what happens when there is no light present."
>
> Finally, the young man asked the professor. "Sir, does evil exist?"
>
> Now uncertain, the professor responded, "Of course as I have already said. We see it every day. It is in the daily example of man's inhumanity to man. It is in the multitude of crime and violence everywhere in the world. These manifestations are nothing else but evil."
>
> To this the student replied, "Evil does not exist, sir, or at least it does not exist unto itself. Evil is simply the absence of God. It is just like darkness and cold, a word that man has created to describe the absence of God.
>
> God did not create evil. Evil is the result of what happens when man does not have God's love present in his heart. It's like the cold that comes when there is no heat or the darkness that comes when there is no light."
>
> The professor sat down.
>
> The young student's name? Albert Einstein.

Does it shock or unnerve you to claim that each one of us is essentially good, including my father or Hitler? Perhaps. However, if you find the courage to look deeply enough you may discover the light in them is identical to the light in you.

On some level I knew as a small child that everyone was good. Goodness is who we are beyond dreams of pain and death, and we cannot be hurt, for we live forever as one.

"Child of Light, you know not that the light is in you. Yet you will find it through its witnesses, for having given light to them they will return it. Each one you see in light brings your light closer to your awareness."

—*A Course in Miracles* (T-13.VI.10:1-3)

Chapter 5: Good Grief

"You cannot be hurt, and do not want to show your brother anything except your wholeness. Show him that he cannot hurt you and hold nothing against him, or you hold it against yourself."

—*A Course in Miracles* (T-5.IV.4:4-5)

"Life on earth is a series of losses." I've found this sentiment to be a harsh certainty during our earth walk. And the happy news is that underneath all those losses lies your true Self, the part of you that cannot be hurt.

We cannot be hurt. We are the otters of the Universe, a line from *Illusions* by Richard Bach, the first book that introduced me to the concepts of illusion. It was recommended by my youngest brother Martin, who, probably for good reason, disowned himself from the family decades ago. I loved the book, as it depicted spontaneous healing, cloud vaporizing, and the idea that we don't need airplanes to reach great heights. These other-worldly concepts satisfied my imagination and strangely made sense. In my late twenties, I ate it up, claiming this was my favorite book of all time, for on some level I knew that a world filled with such pain couldn't be the work of a loving God.

One of the last spankings I sustained was at sixteen years of age. As I braced myself against the top bunk frame while I was whipped with the belt for what seemed like a dozen lashings, now totally humiliated, I swore I would not let my father see me cry or beg for him to stop ever again. Though I winced I did not shed a single tear and didn't even try to protect myself with my hands to ward off the full impact of the blows. I walked away from that beating upright and strong instead of slouched and whimpering, vowing never to cry again. Incidentally, it worked against me in the long run because for decades, I couldn't cry no matter what happened. Like a well gone dry, I could no longer shed a tear.

Billy led the procession of what would be three more buckling losses. Our mother passed away in the midst of divorce proceedings immediately after coming out of surgery to remove a blood clot from her leg, five years after Billy's death almost to the day. Some say she never recovered from losing her eldest son on top of the strain of an unwanted divorce. Amongst her possessions I discovered a touching five-page letter from Chet Mayer, the caretaker at Sunset View Cemetery in Eagle. Mom had a way of saving clippings, quotes, and poems that were meaningful to her. She had never spoken to anyone about Chet's heartfelt written words. It is my understanding that she couldn't find where Billy was buried since there was only a tin marker on his grave at the time. A temporary metal stake courtesy of the funeral home I suppose. Upon finding Chet's letter, I was so moved that I immediately wrote back to thank him for his kind words.

In response to my letter he wrote, "I still remember very clearly your mother looking for her son's grave. I was so willing to help your mother. I felt so very sorry for her. She was sobbing so hard she couldn't talk. I wanted to do more for her but couldn't. When she found the grave of her son I don't know how long she spent on her knees crying. Still I could do nothing. If I remember right, Billy took his own life. Too bad he didn't have counseling if that was the case. One can always think of things to do after it is too late. Sorry she and Billy didn't get to spend more time together in this world. They are no doubt together now. I was also very sorry to hear of her death. She was so young. There is so much sadness in this old world that goes unattended."

Dad was whisked away in a fleeting four months after a cancer diagnosis eight years later. And just when I didn't think our family could take any more, my fun-loving little sister Jackie was killed in a mysterious alcohol-related hit-and-run incident, still unsolved, just five years after we lost our father.

At thirty-three-years young it's no wonder that deep sorrow colored my life. For many years I was in constant fear of who was going to die next. This led me to become like a mama bear trying to maneuver her cubs across a raging river, constantly obsessed with the safety and health of my loved ones. My family grew wary of my round-the-clock worriment and insinuations that I knew what was best for their livelihood. This fretful behavior has brought me unnecessary suffering, sleep loss, stolen peace, and lost opportunities for joyous, precious moments with loved ones. On top of the underlying mountain of buried fear and grief, this obsession with their safety was alienating me from a family who just wanted to be loved and accepted for who they were. I gained a reputation as a control freak, which cut like a knife. Alas, I felt misunderstood by the very people I was afraid of losing.

Remarkably, though, grief seemed to melt away when I could feel Billy's athletic strength in my own body while doing pull-ups, or when a sudden gust of wind brought my attention to a wisp of spiraling leaves, I'd distinctly become aware of Jackie's tender and dynamic presence. And when I remembered the love exchanged when my father caressed my thumbnail with his or when I came across a little red-haired girl in the neighborhood riding her tricycle—the spitting image of a childhood photo of my mother—I was prompted to look back with awe at this timeless wink and say "thank you."

No one can take away the love you shared. That is forever. This is where memory serves us, truly. It was mom's joyful singing almost every morning, not her world of dark depression. It was her joy and dad's, too, for the love we received lifted us above the discord at home. On my earth walk I have uncovered a comforting truth: Love never dies.

Honor Your Experience

"When you choose to make this exchange, you will simultaneously exchange guilt for joy, viciousness for love, and pain for peace."

—*A Course in Miracles* (T-5.VI.2:7)

Railing at the powers that be, "This shouldn't be happening" is the epitome of fighting what is playing out before you as you unwisely deny your experience in hopes of sidestepping inner pain.

The bottom line is, unpleasant things do happen, and resisting the unbearable is part of the first stage of grief—shock. In my mind this stage is a miraculous opening in the space between this world and divinity. An entryway to a higher realm. This includes dizzying confusion, and it is completely natural and normal. It is your psyche's way of protecting you.

Simply identifying the emotion relieves it to some degree. In the same vein, when we name the emotion it's the perfect opportunity to dive in and heal at a deeper level.

Shock, denial, anger, depression, and acceptance arise with great loss, usually in this order. And yet years later, I will experience their residue again in no particular order at all. It's absolutely natural to resist pain, which is actually a healthy reaction to loss of any kind. The grieving process isn't over in one pass and may resurface again years later or on an anniversary. This merely indicates there is more residue to welcome and release.

However, grief tends to lessen its hold as time passes. Inner wisdom encourages you to allow yourself to feel what you feel as long as you feel it. It may seem less intense each time it comes back around. Embracing your emotions becomes the doorway to healing and will leave you free of the heavy effects of unprocessed grief.

Unfortunately, we tend to hear comments such as "Don't cry" or "Get over it" from well-meaning friends, which leads to swallowing our emotions. Repression of any emotion can pave the way toward habitual escapism, drowning our sorrows, and, in my case, wanting control of others. As long as we continue this it shall wreak havoc on the quality of our lives. It requires a whole lot of work and energy to push away intense feelings because emotions are perfectly natural and meant to flow. It is so much less tiresome to welcome your feelings with curiosity. This receptive approach is bound to awaken and invigorate your soul.

Often the friend suggesting that you "just move on" has not dealt with his or her own buried grief. When you are feeling it in their presence, it's just a little too close for comfort on a subconscious level, and so they urge you to bury it, not unlike my father stifling our cries when I was a child.

We avoid feeling some emotions at any cost, just like at age sixteen when I swore to not cry when beaten. When I finally allowed the reservoir of stuck emotion to resurface with conscious awareness many years later, it literally freed me. No longer was the natural spillway blocked, and I was free to gently weep again—to embrace all my emotions and realize greater peaks of happiness too.

When we dam up unwanted feelings, it often paves the way toward avoidant behaviors—chronic busyness, overeating, overindulging in media, mind-altering substances—consequently leading to addiction, relationship strife, exhaustion, and dis-ease.

Spiritualizing

"It was meant to be," "Time heals all wounds," "Everything happens for a reason." All of these statements may be true, but to spiritualize loss can be another clever tactic to avoid feeling what you do.

Devastating losses in our lives are designed to bring us back to deeper realms of peace. Those dedicated to spiritual growth and inner calm will discover in the pages to come how to find relief from the unbearable, how to transform pain in an instant, and how embracing rather than resisting emotion can actually heal your heart.

I have allowed the tangled web of confusion that accompanies grief to have its way with me. Sometimes devastating sorrow can be an opening to a world of ineffable peace. It is meant to be welcomed and embraced. I learned that the onslaught of sudden shock and confusion creates an opening that divinity pours through, ushering in healing. I found the gifts are many, including reaching unimagined heights of transcendent joy. Meeting feelings of grief head-on has helped me to make my moments count, to connect with the spirit of those who've left this plane, and to fully enjoy doing nothing of any importance with the people and pets that I love. It has prompted me to take a step back from the need to control outcomes and to instead relish ordinary moments with all whom I encounter.

On my journey I have found that the love we have shared with any being is eternal. When we compassionately hold the space for ourselves to feel surfacing grief for as long as we feel it, the static clears and we can look beyond the perceived disaster by instead focusing our attention on the love shared with those who've passed, as well as the helpers, the neighbors, friends, and strangers who show up to pick up the pieces. They are keeping the tempo of the song of oneness when you forget the melody in the midst of pain by way of their charitable actions. Come back to this instant where the window of healing occurs. Divine alchemy is in full force, and pain is transformed into peace.

> "Life will break you. Nobody can protect you from that, and living alone won't either, for solitude will also break you with its yearning. You have to love. You have to feel. It is the reason you are here on earth. You are here to risk your heart. You are here to be swallowed up. And when it happens that you are broken, or betrayed, or left, or hurt, or death brushes near, let yourself sit by an apple tree and listen to the apples falling all around you in heaps, wasting their sweetness. Tell yourself you tasted as many as you could."

> —Excerpt from *A Painted Drum* by Louise Erdrich

Part II: You Cannot Hide

Chapter 6: She's Come Undone

"Let them all go, dancing in the wind, dipping and turning till they disappear from sight, far, far outside of you. And turn you to the stately calm within, where in holy stillness dwells the living God you never left, and Who never left you."

—*A Course in Miracles* (T-18.I.8:1-2)

It was a tall order and a heavy load to begin the journey of healing generations of dysfunction, especially transcending the mad, violent outbursts that my parents, their parents, and theirs probably endured with antiquated beliefs that forbade talking about such things.

Grasping for a lifeline after enduring such childhood instability as a young adult meant making many, many, mistakes. I truly believed that once I left the sheer need for survival at home and was out of immediate danger I could run my life. However, at my utter consternation, this was not the case. I didn't know what I was headed for.

You can run, but you cannot hide from the ghosts of your past that haunt you. Although fictitious, buried thoughts trigger terror at a cellular level, spiraling into the "poor me's" and victimhood, or worse—unshakable guilt. I tried to hide from them for years, which had me digging my heels deeper into my desperation.

We deal with memories and past experiences in two ways. We either wallow in them, rehashing them and torturing ourselves from our "ain't it awful" stories of days long gone, or we try to outrun our memories, believing if we run fast and far enough it never really happened. However, as long as we cower under the covers from these phantoms and haven't yet discovered another way, they will continue to haunt us and, in my experience, what we refuse to look at can in no way be escaped.

It is all too easy to use mood-altering substances, engage in chronic busyness, or distract ourselves with family, economic, or political melodrama to try to obliterate these unhealed memories. Interestingly, I've observed in myself and others, clients included, how we seem to attract the very circumstances that we're trying so desperately to forget. Is this a test? Are we forsaken, or could this be the universe giving us another opportunity to heal it and grow? In other words, despite our beliefs that the world is against us, perhaps the universe is just inviting us to heal more layers. As the Sufi Proverb states, "A lesson is repeated until learned."

With the prompting of the low mind we resurrect past trauma because our higher Self wants to expose all that is holding us back. Like a paper clip to a magnet we tend to attract, or more accurately project outwardly, what must be healed within, magnetizing similar incidents to us and bringing another fertile opportunity to release, reframe, and rebalance. As an adult I was reenacting perceived trauma unconsciously so that it could finally be healed. In essence, we project the past unhealed trauma onto the now and future and, consequently, draw it in.

"His Voice will teach you how to distinguish between pain and joy, and will lead you out of the confusion you have made."

—*A Course in Miracles* (T-7.X.7:3)

In my desperation to put my past behind me, a twenty-six-year-old divorced mother of two, a dangerous ignorance peppered with a sense of invincibility led me to treacherous ground in the dating scene. Putting myself and my children in harm's way, I wandered into the arms of men who were on the same path of escaping the pain of their past, no doubt hoping I could help them forget just as I'd hoped they could save me, which of course only added to our delusion and served as a mutual diversion of sorts. Perhaps in the same way Jack and Katie, my parents, found each other.

When that didn't work, I'd become obsessed with escaping in front of the television, while trying to binge eat my troubles away. I was unable to properly parent my young children, and although I was there in body, they surely felt abandoned.

Though seeing me as a loving and doting mother, by Jacinda's own account, not only did she witness my explosive outbursts toward her brother, never knowing when I might lose it, but she also observed the men in my life as all important, leaving her forgotten and secondary.

As challenging as single parenting can be, I managed to feed and clothe my children and provide a place to sleep, but I was overcome with fatigue, robbed of any sense of pride or motivation. Our home was more reminiscent of a disaster zone, as it was all I could do to keep up with laundry, raise two children, and do my best to pay the bills. As determined as I was to be a good mom, an empty shell was merely posing as a mother.

When all else had failed, I'd starve myself and exercise until I completely exhausted myself, thinking I could get skinny enough to attract Mr. Right. Certainly this would solve all my problems and somehow erase my past. *Look to the future*, I thought. Oh, but wait a minute, hadn't I tried this before? That's about the time alcohol found its way into the picture. Evidently disordered eating, including bulimia, wasn't sufficient to push away the pain of my past. Let's have fun. Too bad that meant frequenting the Brush Creek Saloon.

My quest for good times never doused the traumatic memories either. I often left my two precious children with teen babysitters who were unkind and abusive, unbeknownst to me. Horrified when this came to my attention, I was crushed with guilt like a tin can. My opinion of myself sank into the depths. Although my comparatively short plunge into the party scene lasted a half dozen years, it took a toll on every aspect of my life. I would eventually use pills, downers from the dental office where I was employed. My coworkers said, "Take one! This will really get rid of your headache." And soon I was having imaginary headaches every day.

Is it possible to reconcile past trauma? Can we really succeed at ignoring it? The choice to wallow or outrun it does not free us or heal us in any way. So, what is the alternative?

It seems each of us has life lessons to learn—what I affectionately refer to as earth school—and must experience going the wrong way a few times before we discover a better way, the way of true healing, love, and light. This scenario is played out differently but cast with the same problem. What is the problem? Is it our perception of the past, our belief that it was somehow our fault, that we are destined for victimhood? Or perhaps the mad idea that we are essentially no good, worthless, and deserve punishment?

"When you feel guilty, remember that the ego has indeed violated the laws of God, but *you* have not. Leave the 'sins' of the ego to me. . . . until you change your mind about those whom your ego has hurt, the Atonement cannot release you. While you feel guilty your ego is in command, because only the ego can experience guilt. *This need not be.*"

—*A Course in Miracles* (T-4.IV.5:1-6)

Crack of Light

"Light does not attack darkness, but it does shine it away."

—*A Course in Miracles* (T-8.IV.2:10)

Everyone's journey back to God is unique. When that brutal turning point came to a head, I had survived a devastating divorce, done my best to raise my two children, experimented with alcohol and drugs, escaped into disordered eating, and engaged in extreme exercise rituals. Somehow, in the midst of the bedlam, three divine interventions showed up before I was twenty-four. Proof that the universe was indeed conspiring for my ultimate good.

Firstly, I attended open Alcoholics Anonymous meetings with my first husband Kelley and regularly attended Al-Anon meetings—support for those who love an alcoholic. This opened the door to the concepts of the twelve steps.

Secondly, I was introduced to meditation by my therapist, forming a consistent spiritual practice that would carry me through the rest of my life. Dedicating myself to meditation was a thread that kept God in my life no matter how far I drifted.

Lastly, I happened upon the book *Love Is Letting Go of Fear*. This tiny book introduced me to the basic concepts of *A Course in Miracles*. My jogging buddy and coworker, Margie, and I, on our forty-minute commute to the Orthopedic Clinic in Vail, would routinely put into practice the daily lessons in this simple yet profound book.

Today, I look at these milestones as nothing short of divine intervention that, in spite of my delusion, I somehow found a way to receive. Thank goodness I got a wake-up call due to attending those open meetings. I realized I had very real addiction problems and finally admitted I needed help too. I'd like to say my past broke its power over me with the cessation of mood-altering substances, and though the pink cloud, the exhilaration experienced during the first stages of recovery was short-lived, it provided a necessary lifeline to begin my journey of recovery.

It is my humble conclusion that there is no hope for us to move through the maze of lies toward true healing while drowning our sorrows. You can want to become healthier, but it doesn't happen by ignoring the warning signs.

The principles of the A.A. program introduced me to the concept of ego, which was very different from the textbook version that I learned in school, which says you need ego to succeed in the world. I began pondering a new definition of ego and set about linking myself to a higher power that I couldn't yet call "God," but I knew something was there.

This simple acronym says it all: Edging God Out. EGO, as A.A. describes it, pendulates from pride's "I got this," while whistling in the dark, "I need no one. I can handle my problems on my own," followed by the shame of "I am contemptible, lower than dirt, and unworthy of God's help." This is the perpetual feedback loop that surely keeps us stuck.

The fellowship of Alcoholics Anonymous acted initially as a lifeline and then became a bridge to exploring and expanding into deeper spiritual philosophies. My entry into the rooms of

A.A. arrived just in the nick of time because my finger was running out of people to blame for my woes. It had to be, for there before me was a room of once-hopeless addicts in recovery who were presently contributing to society and experiencing more moments of real happiness and freedom one day at a time. Living life with integrity on life's terms.

"Alcoholism," known as a spiritual disease, isn't picky and stems from looking for security, love, and inner peace in all the wrong places. Professionals, stay-at-home or working-from-home moms and dads, and those from all walks of life were represented at this meeting, and they embodied in living color a genuine happiness and liberation they had never known before, and I had surely in my entire life never before witnessed.

Over the course of a year or more, working through the twelve steps with Jan, my sweet-as-honey, soft-spoken but painfully honest sponsor, we completed A.A.'s step five of admitting my wrongs, which brought me to a place of responsibility at last. This was no easy feat. To my horror, the required step work forced me to face my mistakes. In my mind, my greatest fear came true. In order to get back my life, I'd been sentenced to walk through a hollow of guilt and confront a fiery dragon intent on destroying me. Only a miracle could get me through the searing heat and begin the journey of self-forgiveness. If I could face my mistakes squarely, I could amend them. This was the impetus for change. At long last the act of asking the God of my understanding to do for me what I couldn't do for myself, with Jan holding my hand, brought me through the dragon's lair to ground zero—the point of power unscathed. I could finally take in the fresh air of freedom that I'd longed for my whole life.

Why is taking responsibility so important? Because blame doesn't work. Even though you are certain someone attacked you, that kind of retaliatory mindset is precisely what traps you into doing the same things over again while expecting different results. What power did I have while languishing in the atrocities that seemed to permeate my childhood? As long as I remained in the grips of victimhood I could not move forward toward a life of joy and happiness. This world offered no "bys." I still had to pay rent and make a living. To continue to wallow in or shrink from the past was no longer an option.

A Miracle

"As host to the ego, you believe that you can give all your guilt away whenever you want, and thereby purchase peace."

—*A Course in Miracles* (T-15.X.6:1)

I am happy to report that several years into my recovery, a miracle occurred when I'd thoroughly reworked the twelve steps, specifically on codependency, love, and control addiction, with Betsy, another amazing sponsor. It was as if I'd been endowed with x-ray vision, for I could now see men coming a mile away. Arrogant, self-absorbed admirers now had an unmistakable neon light on their forehead flashing STOP! From that point on I heeded the warning and walked the other way.

Like a moth to a flame I used to gravitate toward the men who were unkind, cocky, and domineering. Something carried over from the irrational belief that it was my job to fix my father, formulating the insane conclusion that if I let someone hurt me enough, they might get well. How weird is that? Thankfully, this unhealthy pattern shifted after that step work. The men were still showing up in my life, but I had developed a sensor that reminded me I could not help or fix anyone, especially at my own expense.

The attraction was growing dim as I let go of an old pattern and, after some time, those slippery men stopped coming around. I was free from the mad compulsion toward entanglement with the delusion that I could fix another, which in actuality is just another form of wanting control. When I was finally able to forgive myself, I no longer drew in painfully rocky relationships. After all, isn't the art of healing God's realm? Looking back at this as I'm writing now, it strikes me as outlandishly bizarre, to say the least.

Stable, healthier men started to show up in my life. A girlfriend introduced me to a kind and more conscious gentleman. Though he wasn't the one for me, I realized, contrary to my beliefs at the time, there were some wonderful men out there. Not long after, an easygoing, friendly acquaintance in the A.A. program who attended many of the same meetings that I did, whom I had no romantic interest in before, invited me to a Neil Young concert. I fell in love that very evening. Even though I'd told everyone we were just friends. Somehow, I had overlooked his grounded masculinity and uncommon intelligence. That evening I recognized a warmth and strong sense of loyalty in his magnetic blue eyes. Not surprisingly, Dwayne and I were married, a couple years after I cleaned up my side of the street with regard to my peculiar relational behaviors.

For those to whom this strange pattern seems inconceivable, I've included this poem, which I wrote while still in the clutches of what I refer to as "wanting" love and control addiction. Looking back now, this disorder is reminiscent of my parents' misdirected beliefs in their desperation for inner calm that they would find salvation in each other. It's ironic, really, since in truth, the sense of security that each of us is seeking can only be found within.

"Man – Diction"

Ripping inward for the truth
This cycle called life
Pulls me up by my roots

In utter agony I cry,
My desperate search
Who, what, when, and why?

Each diversion gets even worse
Deranged I cling,
To this nightmarish curse

Frantically I fan the flame
Keep passion alive
Broken, bewildered, and flooded with shame

The terror strikes again, it ends
Now what will replace
The false connection he sends?

I pretend like it's okay
And swallow my tears
It's just another day.

Exhausted, no more, I won't
Keep pretending
Love I thought you had, you don't

But let history speak
Again, over again
Same story, different leak

I can't keep plugging it up
The void is too great
Will I die an empty cup?

All I know is to recover
Why do I want
What I could never win over?

Better to sever all ties
And wipe the slate clean
Than to live with endless lies.

I would rather be alone
With my anguished growth
Than to be bitterly stoned.

Great Spirit give me strength
Come and fill my heart
Alone I go to no lengths

Carry me through this sheer fear
I'll lose my footing
And fall forever . . . , for years

Oh, God. I'm madly afraid
To fully let go . . .
Rely on Your power amidst the blaze.

I'm willing to trust, I pray
The only One whose
Connection forever stays.

And with this leap are many gifts
Through faith I see them
Rising through the sand they'll sift.

Chapter 7: What's Normal Anyway?

"He whispers of His home unceasingly to you. For He would bring you back with Him, that He Himself might stay, and not return again where He does not belong, and where He lives an outcast in a world of alien thoughts."

—*A Course in Miracles* (W-182.7:4-5)

I tried to be normal. I yearned to be like other people, and above all else I didn't want anyone to know of the inconceivable abuse and grief that I'd endured, lest I be shunned, avoided, or considered some piteous outcast. My desperate attempts to hide my past and be like others was always motivated by the fear of exclusion. Undeniably the decision to adhere to the twelve steps got the ball rolling in the right direction, along with the preceding years of talk therapy, which evolved into neurolinguistic programming (NLP) therapy intended to enhance self-awareness and, more recently, eye movement desensitization and reprocessing (EMDR), both of which were instrumental in releasing trauma. My conclusion: Finding inner peace and purpose in life while outrunning the past is like carrying a ball and chain while ascending Mount Everest on roller skates. In my humble opinion, it cannot be done.

We are being called to evolve, for all of our past is unreal, yet we form stories of affection and attachment and, on the other end of the spectrum, aversion, and disbelief and want to push them away without examination. The stories we cling to from days gone by do not define us or make up who we are. Nor are they a reflection of who we are. Whether we can't let go of the past due to judging it, cherishing it, or being haunted by it, nonetheless, we remain locked in a dance with our perceptions of the past. The aversion to the past keeps us just as stuck as our attachment to it. In fact, they're just two sides of the same coin. What is needed is a thorough look at our stories.

You probably know of a couple of adult friends, neighbors, or family members who keep their connection alive through sheer negativity. In much the same way a balloon has the opposite charge as someone's hair, which will stand up and stretch out toward the balloon, two electrical points can stay activated by resistance. Their connection to each other remains strong through the like charges.

All these rivals can do is gossip about the other or engage in mini battles, bolstering their case that it is they who have been wronged. Like bull elks they are still locking horns, for the "other" is still the focal point of their thoughts, and they find themselves preoccupied with the very personality that disgusts them. And in the case of long-held resentment, the "other" is often totally unaware of it. The secret no one can see is it is the defects they have hidden in themselves that mimic the very behaviors in their nemesis who pushes their buttons. We are convinced dissension is unavoidable.

On this earth walk, what we may experience as normal is, unfortunately, loss, death, and disappointment. The world we made, born of fantasy and suppression, is bound to show up sooner or later—a reflection of our own mistaken belief that we are guilty and have done wrongly, accompanied by the terror that someone will find out and discover our defects. It rarely occurs to us that everyone else is doing whatever it takes to fit in too. This world is filled with past misfortune and soul-stirring regrets. The forecast is a dreadful one to be sure. In this scenario we become consumed with what's going to go wrong next. Just listen to the news. As noted previously, we come into this world with a strong lingering suspicion that we are inadequate and unworthy. We cannot help but project this belief outwardly. This extrapolation plays out before us exactly as we imagined, confirming our worthlessness and justifying our persecution. Ego has us right where it wants us. Some go through life defending themselves by blaming external circumstances, while others are taken hostage by this fallacious belief.

This is not so much a psychological issue as a spiritual issue in my mind. It goes much deeper, for wanting to figure it out, fix it, or solve it is just another carrot the ego dangles to keep us apart from our own true healing. Until we reconcile this, we perpetuate it. We undo it by becoming mindful and waking up, so to speak, identifying it and diving into it, as terrifying as that sounds. When we bring light to that belief, whether good or bad, we open the door to healing. What are we healing? Our misperceptions.

As they say, you cannot heal or fix what you won't first examine. Imagine the emergency room doctor not cutting away the clothing or wiping away the blood and loose tissue from around a compound fracture, averting his eyes while he just wraps it in gauze, or, even more ridiculously, amputating the appendage.

In my experience the victim mentality of looking at the past floods through the body's eyes with strong emotions. Egoic stories that you've hidden away are instantly resurrected and cannot help but once again be projected. Like an avalanche it all comes crashing down upon you with no hope of escape. Unbeknownst to you, your current demise ironically holds your release from it.

What to Do?

"Across this bridge, as powerful as love which laid its blessing on it, are all dreams of evil and of hatred and attack brought silently to truth."

—*A Course in Miracles* (W-134.11:1)

It may seem like weakness at first glance. However, the first empowering step in my experience is always to ask for help. Release the emotion in a healthy way. Reframe the stories that stimulate the emotion and, most importantly, build and fortify your connection with Source. Rebalance your life. Access your intuition. Pray, meditate, talk to angels.

Amidst the tranquil hush of humility, the right people, practitioners, and books show up. The universe is calling for each of us to heal all the lies that stand in the way of realizing our ultimate goodness and the truth of who we really are—perfectly innocent, infallible, and immortal. With the slightest willingness, a thousand angels rush in. Isn't it funny how within the abyss of hopelessness faith blooms?

Have you had a spiritual experience? Perhaps an incident that went beyond human understanding, such as evading serious injury or death or an inexplicable monetary gain in the nick of time. You're dumbfounded at how this could have happened in the first place.

In my mind, a spiritual experience cuts through the fog of insanity like a knife. I've hung on to something ineffable that cannot be touched or explained while in the depths of seeming hopelessness. Words fail to describe. It is felt within at a deep level, like an awakened ancient memory. It is a distinct awareness of another realm so very unlike the dream world. It transcends the concept of time. No one can take it away, and it will anchor you all the days of your walk on earth and beyond.

Grand Examples

Have you ever had to live on faith? Do you believe in angels? Have you experienced a miracle? Feeding my children, paying bills, and finding employment immediately after separating from my first husband seemed at the time impossible, for I only had a part-time job and literally lived day by day on faith. I prayed a lot. To my amazement each time a bill would come in or I approached the check-out register, my heart would sink, because I knew I did not have enough to cover expenses. In spite of this, there would appear, to my relief and astonishment, enough cash to cover the groceries or the bill that had arrived in the mail. I cannot tell you how long this lasted, and it was never more than enough; it was always just enough. This boggling phenomenon had me digging in deeper because I didn't know from where this money was coming! Over and over again my wallet provided our basic needs during our hardship until such time as I was able to secure a second part-time job and eventually full-time employment.

One upset at a time, one belief at a time, and one physical concern at a time. Is this normal? Not normal—just earth school lessons and a path we must all have signed up for, whether we've had what we might call extreme "hard times" or a series of inconvenient disappointments. The traumas, tragedies, or tribulations are relative, and what is in front of us is our self-designed curriculum. For through it all, when you dive into and go beyond the stories, emotions, and appearances, you will invariably discover the love, light, and peace that you've always been and will always be.

If something causes upset, it is cause for celebration, for you have just discovered your access point back to peace. Welcome to earth school! At some point in the fog we realize that we enrolled and can now choose to roll up our sleeves and embrace the curriculum.

What, you say? I don't see any curriculum. Dive deeper into the upset, the past that haunts you, and the physical issues that plague you. The "if it's not one thing, it's another" that permeates your world is your customized roadmap back home to the peace that was within you all along.

Normalcy may be hidden in the dawning of awareness. A wake-up call to the fact that we are all one light, one song of love, connected in joy in reality! Life on earth is an opportunity to reawaken unlimited peace, potential, and joy!

"Your worth is established by God. As long as you dispute this everything you do will be fearful, particularly any situation that lends itself to the belief in superiority and inferiority.

—*A Course in Miracles* (T-4.I.7:2-3)

Chapter 8: Not an Ideal World

"To empathize does not mean to join in suffering, for that is what you must *refuse* to understand. That is the ego's interpretation of empathy, and is always used to form a special relationship in which the suffering is shared."

—*A Course in Miracles* (T-16.I.1:1-2)

I remember as a little girl a disturbing inner conviction that something was terribly wrong with this world. It was not ideal, and somehow, it was my job to find that ideal world. I just knew inside that it existed somewhere. As I got older I took this self-imposed responsibility more seriously. In my mind it was up to me to make things better, and that's when I began to sacrifice myself for others and fall to pieces when tragedy struck this world.

Many of us have been under the delusion that we are entitled to a life of ease, happiness, and inner peace, and these wonderful states are supposed to be experienced effortlessly. As we've all encountered the hard knocks that come while we reside in this realm, most of us have found the opposite is truer. Life on earth, as noted earlier, appears to be a series of drama, misfortune, and upset. We find ourselves asking what's wrong instead of what's right. We look for the next problem and set ourselves up to expect the worst because maybe it will lessen the blow of being blindsided by yet another disappointment. Or worse, we drift into blaming ourselves while ruminating for hours in bed about what's wrong with us. Time better spent getting our beauty sleep. Don't you agree?

Enter the infamous Winnie the Pooh character Eeyore, who, probably with his melancholic attitude, was only protecting himself from the next string of unasked-for circumstances. We can spend years sinking into cynicism like Eeyore. Unfortunately, this attitude smothers creativity as well as a sense of connection and overall wellness. Just ask Lynda, who agreed to share her story.

Lynda is successful in her chosen field, real estate. She is naturally giving and compassionate, and she is valued by others, including her clients and coworkers, for her team spirit and willingness to do what it takes to get a job done. She truly cares. On a good day she knows her value, yet episodes of self-doubt can tip the scales into low self-esteem and waning confidence. And because Lynda feels deeply, she finds herself being pulled into the iniquities of this world, the countless problems of her friends as well as family discord.

She is strong, for unconditional servitude takes great strength of spirit and mind, strength beyond this world, but of herself she can no longer continue this way. When the need to try and correct all the wrongs in her world finally caught up with Lynda, her body did its best to compensate by turning to food, shopping, or other indulgences. These indulgences only tipped the scales further and threw her into an emotional tailspin.

Leading with unbridled compassion is draining and burdensome, and Lynda was simply unable to maintain the light that she shines in others' lives. Spent with nothing left to give, she secretly had fantasies of giving up and running away from it all. Lost, anxious, and desperate to end this madness, she finally hit the wall when she began to experience serious health issues, including debilitating fatigue. Now she was the one who needed help. In time she was led to holistic solutions, and today Lynda is vibrant, and lights up the world with her gifts of sensitivity and caring, but with one difference. She has learned to slow down, get quiet, and focus on the miracle of oneness by listening to the wisdom within.

Her commitment to change started with awareness, which sparked the willingness to ask for help. With a single decision her healing path unfolded before her. Now she is bubbling with vitality and enthusiasm. She has newfound clarity and has attained a calmness within while maintaining an almost effortless balance in all areas of her life.

Having had a spiritual awakening of sorts, Lynda was divinely guided to drop her pride and receive this message: Let the Holy Spirit empathize through you while seeing beyond the illness or troubles of another and instead focus on the light and love in them that never dies.

This imperceptible practice yielded monumental results. Although imperceptible, it not only reignited the eternal light within the one for whom she was concerned but simultaneously strengthened the light of oneness within Lynda too. She came to understand that we best serve our highest good by exercising our right to choose to focus on the celestial thread that runs through each of us despite appearances—the essence of love that unifies us. The love that we are beyond whatever the body seems to experience.

"Yet of this you may be sure; if you will merely sit quietly by and let the Holy Spirit relate through you, you will empathize with strength, and will gain in strength and not in weakness."

—A Course in Miracles (T-16.I.2:7)

In this world we long for ideal circumstances and kind exchanges. We believe all imperfections must be fixed, and we want, most of all, to change the world, fortifying our notions that the world is indeed lacking. Our egoic mind prods us with thoughts such as maybe the ideal world is just around the corner. Major world-changing attempts have been made by known and unsung heroes throughout the millennia.

We spend money, time, and energy preoccupied with what is wrong with this world and how we might transform it. However, if we choose instead to implement Lynda's sacred message, we could do more for oneness by healing our misperceptions to pave the road back to a harmonious reality, more than your money, time, or energy could ever do. By all means give when you are moved to do so. I'm not suggesting you side-step your intuition and don't do what you are inspired to do, for inspired action is of God.

Because we live in a less-than-ideal world, many of us feel compelled to change things for the better. And if we don't get on the bandwagon to change things, ego goes for the throat. "Don't you care?" it chants. This effectively keeps us locked into looking outside of ourselves for the solution when it can only be found within.

Have You No Compassion?

"The peace of God is shining in me now. This light can not be lost. Why wait to find it in the future, or believe it has been lost already, or was never there?"

—*A Course in Miracles* (W-188.2:1-2)

I have countless examples of how my choice to connect with another's light rather than buying into their current so-called wrongs or drama helped them and me more than I could have imagined. Now, I trust the gifts of looking past another's misery are received regardless of seeing with my physical eyes an immediate shift. At first glance, I may have been perceived as cold, distant, and without compassion, but I knew from previous encounters the awesome power of the choice to extend love. For we cannot be hurt because, in reality, we are fun-loving, creative eternal beings, and the love and light that we are in truth cannot but survive.

Whenever you feel helpless, when your best friend loses her job, a family member is going through a painful divorce, or during another world crisis, pause before you jump in to save the day or give in to a loved one's commiseration and instead ask for higher vision to find the light in them beyond their perceived predicament—the beauty in the real world now. This is true compassion because you are seeing them beyond the illusion of pain, envisioning their higher Self and allowing Spirit to heal through you. This is your key to freedom.

It may not be an ideal world. However, it is the perfect world to grow spiritually—customized just for you to come back to the peace you never left. Like Lynda, I was stuck in wanting to understand why this world isn't perfectly ideal on the one hand and feeling obligated to fix it on the other. The ego cruises on this ruse. As you will uncover in the next chapter, there is another way. A way that showers you and all whom you encounter with loving-kindness.

Chapter 9: Fix or Forgive

"For forgiveness literally transforms vision, and lets you see the real world reaching quietly and gently across chaos, removing all illusions that had twisted your perception and fixed it on the past. The smallest leaf becomes a thing of wonder, and a blade of grass a sign of God's perfection.

—*A Course in Miracles* (T-17.II.6:2-3)

Because we inhabit an unideal world, it's tempting to assume, like me, that it's our job to fix it. As parents, teachers, and leaders it is easy to believe that we're supposed to make everything okay for our children. We've all experienced being parented in one form or another, and some of us are parents. Parents are human beings, not machines. Mistakes will be made even in the most perfect of circumstances. We spend energy and time blaming our parents or blaming ourselves for the pains our children may have endured. In this world of seeming chaos, confusion, and scarcity, it is impossible to protect our children from harsh events or fulfill their every need.

The bottom line is we are getting nowhere carrying this heavy burden because we cannot fix this world. But there is a point of power in this illusory world. A point of power called forgiveness, and it's a big stretch to disengage from the need to make things right to the grace of forgiving them.

In this chapter we'll dive deeper into the concept of real forgiveness. I'll also explain the difference that I've come to discover through my own bruises from banging my head up against the world of illusion to find that trying to fix things keeps us stuck.

Moving toward principled adulthood comes with the realization that you can only change yourself. Few relish the idea of inner work. Nonetheless, to sift through and disentangle long-cherished stories of blame and vengeance opens the door to self-honesty and toward the basic sovereignty to take responsibility for what you *can* change. We can stop hiding from ourselves and reclaim the power of decision. Growth as we enter adulthood is about letting go of blame, anger, and sadness to instead discover the healing salve only forgiveness offers. I have found it imperative to form a relationship with a power greater than ourselves for such a journey. This requires implementing practices that help you to access your higher Self. As the serenity prayer hastens, accept the things you cannot change and ask for the courage to change the things you can.

"Forgiveness sweeps away distortions, and opens the hidden altar to the truth. Its lilies shine into the mind, and call it to return and look within, to find what it has vainly sought without. For here, and only here, is peace of mind restored."

—*A Course in Miracles* (W-336.1:4-6)

How hard the ego fights to keep its delusion of control. I wanted to fix the past without first forgiving it. This played out during the first few years of sobriety in order to keep me imprisoned in my world of hell, as my ego got very inventive. I experienced a stupefying series of hard lessons, including relationship drama, constant financial struggles, a second divorce, family heartache, two teenagers with serious issues of their own, and continued disordered eating prompted by and resulting in self-loathing—a vicious cycle that manifested as the irrational need to change my body with the next beauty product, compulsive exercise, and the latest dieting trends. The more extreme, the better. My father didn't have to beat me up anymore, for I was doing a pretty good job of it myself. Frankly, the past I was desperately trying to outrun didn't just go away with sobriety. Sobriety was but a necessary prerequisite.

True forgiveness frees us. Trying to fix the things of this realm imprisons us and is yet another diversion in the world of ego.

A World of Duality

"Fear condemns and love forgives. Forgiveness thus undoes what fear has produced, returning the mind to the awareness of God."

—*A Course in Miracles* (W-46.2:2-3)

Wanting to fix the past, or at least explain it to relieve guilt, to make it so you can never be hurt again, and to make it so no one else is hurt unjustly is distracting, to say the least. Protect the innocent. Step in when someone appears to bully another, and on a larger scale, such as when countries treat their citizens unfairly or wage wars without provocation. The trouble is trying to fix the world of duality, in which black and white, ups and downs, and right and wrong will never end. The small mind's incessant need to preoccupy you has succeeded at keeping your hands tied and away from realizing the love that surrounds you. Just when you seem to make progress something else goes awry. In this realm, history simply repeats itself. In the whole of recorded history, has there ever been peace on earth, a time of no unrest? Has there ever been a time when the elders did not complain about the uncivilized behaviors of the younger generation? This is not new, as it's been recorded since Plato's time.

Plato was heard to remark, "What is happening to our young people? They disrespect their elders, they disobey their parents. They ignore the law. They riot in the streets, inflamed with wild notions."

Sound familiar? Our grandparents said it about our parents, our parents said it about us, and to be honest, have you recently criticized your daughter-in-law or perhaps your nephew? If we could have changed this dynamic, wouldn't we have by now, somewhere in the last thousand years or so? That's just it. The belief that we can change or fix this world of chaos is false. It cannot be attained because this world of illusion is a product of ego.

Suppose for a moment there is another approach. During many *A Course in Miracles* philosophical group discussions, the question of making right an injustice versus forgiving it came up over and over again. The ego is cunning, to be sure, because as soon as we dip into the need to fix something, are we not now attempting to play God and bypass true wisdom? The lower mind taunts that it is your job to fix the wrongs that appear on this earth. Imagine stepping back from the pompous notion that you can fix or change things and instead ask to see things in a new light, favoring a more intuitive understanding. With the slightest willingness to yield to greater wisdom, you've tapped into a power beyond this world.

Oh, but it is challenging to disengage from the belief that I must find a way to fix or change a situation, to demand things be done differently, or that it's my responsibility to rectify all the inequities in this world. The need to forgive implies passed judgement and literally means to give up, release, and let go of resentment, to give up any claim to be compensated for the hurt or loss we believe we have suffered. Belief is not fact.

An ancient Greek definition derived from the word "charizomai" means to give unconditional forgiveness, which essentially means to give up our judgment of another. It suggests letting go, separating the offender from the offense, and recognizing that the misdeed is past and the time for healing is at hand. I resonate with this last definition largely because, in truth, we cannot be hurt, and letting go of the belief that we've been offended ushers in mutual healing. Our power lies in shifting our perceptions rather than mindlessly becoming hell-bent on trying to make others pay. Moreover, it serves only to distract us from what is real, from our perfection and power now. Don't you agree this is a better place from which to live? We try to fix the problem by doling out punishment, taking the role of judge and jury, and thus lose the spiritual healing with which the ripples of forgiveness grace us.

Passive or Powerful?

"Every loving thought is true. Everything else is an appeal for healing and help, regardless of the form it takes. Can anyone be justified in responding with anger to a brother's plea for help? No response can be appropriate except the willingness to give it *(love)* to him, for this and only this is what he is asking for."

—*A Course in Miracles* (T-12.I.3:3-6)

With a mere request, we can rise above this ego trap. Can you truly save another by climbing down into the gutter of misery with him? In the case of a drowning, authorities warn to call for emergency help. Do NOT attempt a rescue by entering the water as you will be endangering yourself. After all, what good would it do either of you if you're flailing in the gutter too?

The ego is a master at running interference, so you hesitate to ask for guidance. With its continuous monologue the small mind lulls you to sleep when it's time to take inspired action.

That action can be as simple as asking for the strength to take the next right step in the moment. The maze of rationalizations and circular thought flood the mind, and the dust the ego stirs up, the smoke and mirrors it conjures, can seem alluring, attractive, and seemingly the only course of action when all you want to do is maintain the status quo.

Give up the temptation to save the world and rise above illusion to that which never dies—the love that unifies us. Just as in my story of abuse, I clearly remember making a pact with my siblings, where each of us swore never to forgive my father, which probably laid the groundwork for future internal pain and dysfunction. Yet it's a choice to recede again into the gutter with ego thoughts of "ain't it awful" or "how could anyone possibly recover from this kind of horror." I am incapable of fixing the past, but I have the means to forgive it. A part of me can see my father in fear and calling for love. With the help of Spirit, I am capable of looking past his mistakes, forgiving the fear that drove his actions to the light and love that exists in him.

Since in reality there is no time, the miracle of forgiveness prevails, and the love that channels through me heals us both simultaneously. As noted earlier, the past can be healed now, defying space and time. I have relinquished the vain idea that I can fix anything and have instead surrendered to the only Power that heals through my willingness to see past my muddled perceptions. I have, in effect, stepped my ego out of the way so true healing may be realized.

This, my fellow travelers, is true empowerment—plugging into Source. This is our only power in this confusing world. The power to decide. To make another choice, to brush away and move beyond illusory judgmental stories and to see the past differently. For the light within is the most powerful gift you possess in reality, and the decision to ask for the strength to channel that light truly dissolves a world of senselessness.

"Fantasies are all undone, and no one and nothing remain still bound by them, and by your own forgiveness you are free to see."

—*A Course in Miracles* (T-17.II.3:5)

I am still working on this labor of love, namely forgiveness, daily. When emotions or disturbing memories arise from the perceived instability I endured as a child, I ask for a little help to dive in and let go as I allow my heart to heal and for the strength to also extend grace to those I thought had hurt me. Retroactive healing is timeless, not just for me but for all who came before.

On the other hand, when we let go of the need to fix or change things, we are making a choice to plug into Source and extend forgiveness. Not the antiquated definition of forgive, which means to ignore a wrong, but by contrast, "to see past it." Not because we are being holier than thou but because we have realized that our perceptions are distorted. In essence we forgive for what was not done, not for what was done. Love and only love governs this universe and is all that is real. Put simply, we are forgiving the small mind's need to pass judgment by making the choice to look past our skewed perceptions.

Releasing our stubborn attachments allows for higher wisdom to rush in, and with that, misunderstandings dissolve and a new and fresh outlook bursts through. Freedom lies in allowing God to do for us what we cannot do for ourselves by applying this all-inclusive version of forgiveness. Love is asking us to look beyond, see past, let go, and extend grace by acquiescing to a power greater than ourselves. You see it's the stories of condemnation in our heads that cause unyielding attitudes. Know that these attachments are nothing more than static electricity and can only temporarily disrupt our journey to peace.

"It is not time we need for this. It is but willingness. For what would seem to need a thousand years can easily be done in just one instant by the grace of God."

—*A Course in Miracles* (W-196.4:3-5)

Chapter 10: The Master Within

"The past is over. It can touch me not. Unless the past is over in my mind, the real world must escape my sight."

—*A Course in Miracles* (W-289.1:1)

The past is the past, and it requires astute awareness to recognize thoughts, emotions, and various physical distractions as cues. The wanting to escape from it all is clear evidence that more residue of the past is surfacing to be uncovered, for healing transcends both time and space.

I have found that the past surfacing in your life now is calling for healing. Healed in this context means, to me, to cease buying into the lies raining down on my world, clearing the way to higher vision for all of us. In my experience what is coming up is an assignment that was missed in our lessons, and once accepted, will become another rung on the ladder toward enlightenment and inner peace, for it is by diving into what disturbs us that surely sets us free.

Unconsciously we allow the residue of "hurts gone by" to seep into our lives, and the past we thought we escaped becomes the backdrop of our lives. It may keep us in fear of the future, of playing small, of overreacting to situations, or of finding ourselves stuck again in the cycle of escapism and chronic busyness.

In essence what we experience in the now, whether it shows up as what we see, hear, or feel before us or leaching old stories that trigger buried trauma, it is showing up right now. It's still the now and is again asking to be addressed now, whether it is playing out in our lives or as a memory in our heads. Rather than clinging to overindulging in food, other substances, escapism tendencies, or dysfunctional relationships, we can find and surrender to the Master within.

How to address it? This is when I make a choice and pray for the courage to take the next step to heal it. I am always directed. Sometimes Spirit leads me to a book, blog, counselor, coach, or group, but as I've grown, it usually directs me to the wisdom within as I've taken the first step by asking for help. No matter how I am directed, it typically requires diving into the disturbance. Is it a nagging thought, overwhelming emotion, bad habit, relationship, or health issue that has gotten my attention? Identifying it by naming it is a vital next step.

To reiterate, with our willingness the past that seems to haunt us begins to dissipate. Its hold has lessened. We are free of another layer of clouds that appear to obscure the light and love in us and around us. The light that is us. We begin to realize the past cannot hurt us, and it is only by diving into the effects of our past, whether they play out inside our heads or in our world in front of us in the moment that we can be free.

Serendipitously, as you grow, you will begin the next lesson, assignment, or layer to complete, each time replacing old beliefs with a beautiful, clean slate and an open mind. Your job is to choose to recognize, welcome, and explore as the next layer presents itself. This includes the panic response of "Oh, no, not this again" or the impulse to push it away for welcoming, and yes, even the acknowledgment of resistance is the way through and back to center.

Always asking for guidance from your inner Teacher, the Master within, leads us back to maintaining open communication with the divine by implementing small practices such as meditation, a walk in nature, and various mundane tasks, like washing the dishes, with complete awareness. By embracing these ordinary moments daily, hourly, and minute by minute, we are no longer falling asleep with the small mind at the wheel.

"Nothing you have ever learned can help you understand the present, or teach you how to undo the past. Your past is what you have taught yourself. Let it all go."

—*A Course in Miracles* (T-14.XI.3:5-7)

As you continue completing your lessons toward love you become lighter, more childlike, and more transparent because, after all, the light that seems to have been dimmed is shining brighter in you and through you. You feel it on the inside, and you and others see it in each other beyond the body's eyes and senses. Thus, the higher Self in others recognizes the eternal love and light in you.

That begs the question of God. If you're like many of us, this topic is confusing. Where do I start and God begin? And how do we reconcile the two? Let's take a closer look at the divine, shall we?

Chapter 11: A Delicate Subject

"This is true, but it is hard to explain in words because words are symbols, and nothing that is true need be explained. However, the Holy Spirit has the task of translating the useless into the useful, the meaningless into the meaningful, and the temporary into the timeless."

—*A Course in Miracles* (T-7.I.6:4-5)

Who or what is God? I often dance around this word, but I am being directed to jump in and hit this mystifying topic like a paratrooper. Earlier I mentioned that we cannot do this kind of spiritual work without help from something greater than ourselves.

God, why did you do this to me? For years I hated God, for I saw God as something to blame, to fear, out to hurt me, and to make my life miserable, believing he deemed me unworthy by damning me to a life of tribulation. Many other holy words offended me as much as the word God at first. Why? Because these words hold a higher vibration and threaten the lower mind. Though still just symbols, they carry a frequency of omnipotence. Suppose it is not you who cringes at certain sacred words but the ego.

Become honest with yourself with regard to your reaction to the word that symbolizes a power greater than yourself. Get curious. Call it what you will—God, Source, Yahweh, Higher

Self, Jehovah, Great Spirit, Allah, Om, Eternal Light, Holy Spirit—for it is the access point to stepping into a higher realm. If you bristle, acknowledge the vibration of resistance in your body, inhale and exhale into it, and after a couple minutes consciously release the resistance.

The spoken word is just air moving past our vocal cords, causing a sound vibration, right? That said, any word that evokes strong emotion is calling for you to heal something inside. I may be reaching a bit here. However, it may serve you to explore further.

Check inside. Allow yourself to dig deeper. Notice any aversion or bristling that you may have as you continue reading, especially to the word "God." You may or may not have a strong reaction. However, if you do, I challenge you to notice the annoyance or irritation within or any other feeling that it evokes. In this way you shall transcend the symbol into pure, unfettered understanding beyond the word itself.

I have found taking the initiative to investigate my fears has led me toward deeper self-understanding. The mere mention of the word God or other pious words could put me immediately on the defensive, yet I have found beneath my initial reaction there is often a gift leading me to greater depths of spiritual connection. If certain sacred words bother you, take note for now because, in this chapter, we will be looking at the hidden gift that comes from resistance.

Oh, the mistakes I've made, but the biggest of them all and most damaging was to believe God is my enemy who punishes, considers us bad, and will abandon us. God did not cause the catastrophes as the ancients believed. It was actually the cycle of fear, revenge, and remorse projected outward that caused the often prophesized disasters.

"Fear of retaliation from without follows, because the severity of the guilt is so acute that it must be projected."

—*A Course in Miracles* (T-5.V.3:11)

As I Understand God

For so long I wondered how God could let others suffer so needlessly, especially children. Was he punishing us? What did I do to bring my early traumas—His wrath—upon me? And why didn't He make my daddy better when I'd prayed so hard? Why did my family, which was so close to me, get taken away one after the other? As I saw it, God was against me, and I had to doubt His existence to make sense of tragedy and usurp the belief that I was doomed to an existence ridden with pain and punishment. I in no way wanted to believe in this deity, let alone worship Him.

When I first walked into the rooms of Al-Anon and Alcoholics Anonymous, they dared use the word God. Could you imagine my bewilderment? It was all I could do not to storm out. They held my hand and encouraged me to keep coming back. And because I had nowhere else to go, I did. My very first Al-Anon sponsor, Jean, an outspoken, wiry, dedicated, wise woman who guided me through the twelve steps, assured me that I didn't have to believe in God and went on to suggest that I make up my own concept of a power greater than myself. This was all the willingness that was required, Jean assured me. At that juncture I couldn't even muster the willingness, as my mind had slammed shut a long time ago. She suggested that I pray for the willingness to be willing. Hmmm . . . the willingness to be willing . . . well, I could do that.

To my surprise the willingness arrived, whereupon I arbitrarily chose a doorknob as my concept of God for the time being due to the fact that I was currently referring to myself as an agnostic. I wasn't completely certain of what that meant, but it sounded sophisticated, rebellious, and a little edgy, so as a twenty-year-old I went with it. In my thwarted perception God had taken everything away from me. Looking back at this today, a doorknob was perfect because it is a symbol of the freedom to choose and shows you how to exit the old and access new places, revealing to us what we couldn't see before. For me it represented a tiny willingness. Yes, indeed, a doorknob represents an opening, a choice, a decision, to either stay or to go and to take one path or another.

Enter the concepts of non-dualism or absolute oneness, such as Buddhism, Taoism, Hinduism, and *A Course in Miracles*. I realized God doesn't see us in this prison of separateness and broken dreams that we made but as we are, in truth, perfectly innocent, infallible, and immortal. Life is oneness. Love is all that is real, and our illusions of fear are just that—illusions in a tiny dream.

In time, God became my friend, and little by little, I gained purity of vision, right action, and the absolute certainty that everyone is good and perfect, just as I somehow understood as a little child. A direct contrast to the churches of organized religion that taught me I should feel this way and shouldn't do that, and that he is good but she is bad. This sounded a lot like my father's credo. In this model my fate was all too dependent on outside opinions and imposed dogma. The spiritual ideas of A.A. allowed a crack of light to seep through originally, and the door of willingness swung open in my quest for a compassionate, loving concept of God. At some point, I cannot remember exactly when, the word God no longer made me cringe.

Religion or Spirituality?

Danielle, a client and colleague in the midst of a life transition, quipped that her religion might be getting in the way of her spirituality. When you review the definitions I offer in the next paragraphs, it becomes obvious how these concepts can be misconstrued.

Religion may impose limits. Traditional religious beliefs and practices with respect to God, based on the interpretations of man on fundamental teachings, often exclude those who do not share the same views. Unfortunately, this causes judgmental attitudes toward others going both ways and serves only to propagate a hostile rift.

Spirituality is, on the other hand, a broad, more inclusive concept with room for many perspectives. We are all one, based primarily on the individual experiencing a direct connection with the sacred. As such, it is a universal human experience—something that links all of us.

For instance, higher Self is a term associated with many belief systems, but its basic premise describes an eternal, omnipotent, and loving being, who is one's real self. I'm sure you've heard before that we aren't humans having a spiritual experience. We are Spiritual Beings having a human experience.

You can't see It, feel It, taste It, or smell It, but you know It's there. Something that carries you through when times are tough. Something within that touches you deeply when looking at a sunset or a thing of utter beauty. It seems somehow elusive.

How do you keep this wonder in your life more consistently? How do you define and unite with Universal Love?

When I use the word God, I use it with reverence, without explanation or excuse, but also with respect for you and your journey, for it is again your experience of awe, of stillness, of peace, love, selflessness, joy, light, immortality, and beauty that defines your use of this sacred word. Use the word that best suits you. Source, Jesus Christ, Abba, Father, Universal Love, Divine Being, Yeshua, or a doorknob.

When my daughter was just four years young the subject of God came up when I asked, "Honey, what does God mean to you?" She pondered the question briefly and piped up with a single word—"Love." Out of the mouths of babes.

Just as a vampire recoils from a blessed cross, the small self shies away from a power greater than itself at all costs. The reason I encourage you to tune in when you hear a word that may ruffle your feathers is because to pause into the vibration, and all that you feel from mild irritation, curiosity, calm, or absolute detest, can actually be freeing. Make it a habit when a sacred word bothers you to observe with acute awareness the inner emotional vibration apart from your thoughts. Get curious for a moment and gently follow your visceral reactions as you let the emotion dissolve to the best of your ability. A softening may occur like a door opening, and that is all that is needed. You may never love certain words, but you'll reverse the aversion or attachment to not loving them and thus free yourself and your mind.

Chapter 12: A Direct Route

"Why should you listen to the endless insane calls you think are made upon you, when you can know the Voice for God is in you?"

—*A Course in Miracles* (T-5.VII.3:1)

As the crow flies, there is no better route to a state of calm and heightened awareness than the practice of meditation. Fortunately, I was instructed to begin a meditation practice when I was twenty by my therapist, though at the time I was oblivious that this was a catalytic turning point in my young life.

In the beginning it was a brief mechanical discipline as I struggled to practice five days a week, no more than that and never exceeding five minutes first thing in the mornings. When we sit still in silence for very long, our buried past has a way of surfacing, making most of us uncomfortable, and so we occupy ourselves with one thing or another. Meditation was difficult, for it brought up so much terror that it was almost impossible to maintain. Despite this I kept my word. A dozen years ago, after decades of gradually increasing meditation to twenty minutes, I turned a corner. Who knows why I kept at it?

A highly respected, spiritually evolved French woman who came to see me every two months for natural wellness solutions was not only open about but boldly spoke of her dependence on Christ at every turn. During her session I spoke about my meditation practice, referring to it as a forced discipline. Michele, who cherished her sacred meditation practice, asked me, "Why do you not see your ritual as a precious bit of time to connect with eternal love?" With her query, I willingly began practicing every single day. Her straightforward question erased my inner dialogue—"I must, I should, I have to"—and transformed it to "I choose, I desire, I want to commune with the sacred thread that is me beyond this body." Her question instantly shifted my perspective, and since then, it has enriched my life seven days a week. Most days I don't want to end this precious time with universal love, even after thirty minutes.

Meditation, dance, enjoying nature, art, music, and myriad creative pursuits are direct links to the divine and bring us closer to our natural state. These periods of allowing the hallowed to pour through you add up, and each is a sacred stepping stone toward perfect peace.

For those of you who want to learn more about implementing a meditation practice, the biggest hurdle is not sitting in silence but consistently practicing. This is mostly because the small mind is cunning and will pressure you with mind chatter, assuring you there is not enough time or you've got too much to do. It resembles a brutish overseer striking you with an invisible whip to keep you chronically striving and driving, all while pointing out that meditation is a waste of time, keeping you intent on what it deems is really important—your busyness. "Besides, you're incapable of meditating," it drones on, "with all those thoughts floating through your head." In truth, meditation is not so much about quieting the mind as it is about becoming aware of the chatter and repeatedly letting it go. Why? Because ego wants to rule your life, and it knows that when you pause and sink into the moment, its fictitious existence vanishes into thin air.

Once I've overcome the negative mind chatter, it helps to have a dedicated spot other than my bed in which to practice. Leaning back or lying down is counterproductive, as you will slip into an alpha state—and meditation is about conscious awareness, not sleeping. It was suggested that I practice first thing in the morning before the day takes me away, thus establishing a calmness and balance for the day ahead.

I sit upright and root my bottom into the chair or mat and elongate my posture like a ballerina, imagining my spine as an antenna, a beam of light extending out the top of my head unto the heavens as I become a silent receiver. I gently close my eyes or leave them half open while softly focusing on a candle or point on the floor. Slowing down the breath, expanding my belly with each in-breath, and contracting it with each out-breath, I count each full breath cycle from one to ten. After three rounds I have deliberately counted a total of thirty breaths to merge with divine wisdom. This opening series of steps transports me into a deeper, more focused meditation.

When distracted by thoughts or a sound or an itch, I acknowledge the intrusion and let the thought breeze by as I release my attachment to the interruption or scratch the itch if necessary and diligently return to my breath. Occasionally, sadness, anger, or anxiety take me away during my practice. As soon as I become alert to the emotion, I acknowledge the sensations it arouses and then let it drift through as a leaf down a stream, repeatedly and gently redirecting my focus back to the breath. It is helpful for me to set a timer. Keep in mind consistency is more important than duration of time. Set your timer for just five minutes to ease into your new habit and, as I was instructed decades ago, practice at least five days per week.

Some days I spend much of this period in silent reflection fielding internal and external interruptions, but other days it seems natural to be with my breath the entire practice. Most days it is a combination of the two. No matter. The results are the same.

"In stillness we will hear God's Voice today without intrusion of our petty thoughts, without our personal desires, and without all judgment of His holy Word."

—*A Course in Miracles* (W-125.3:1)

In the grand scheme behind the things in this world, you are perfectly innocent, as are your fellow travelers, perfect, whole, and complete. What if you knew that fact? Imagine the implications if each and every one of us knew this truth. How secure, how free, and how beautiful would life become as we rediscover the peace beyond belief?

The miracle is that the oneness we so desperately seek is always here, no matter what you think you have or haven't done, or who you think you are or are not. Our true connection is masked by negative mind chatter, overwhelming emotions, and engaging in habitual escapism, which looks a lot like overeating, wasting time on social media, and aimless busyness.

Our ego, the small self, likes to keep us in turmoil and tempts us with juicy, all-consuming, fantastical stories. It is when we take a break from the static in our heads that we find that inner calm.

Isn't it true that all you are really looking for is peace? It may masquerade as wanting security, having more success or money, wanting appreciation, acclaim, better health, or weight loss, or trying to control the environment and even the people we live and work with. However, achieving these desires will not bring you inner peace or that connection with all living things that you are ultimately seeking. This can only be found within.

I have found three practices that nurture our connection to Source. Firstly, meditation is about focused listening inside. It's about receptivity and following the breath. Even one minute serves. Secondly, fully embracing the present moment during the course of your day. Because Spirit exists in the space between breaths, the silence between sounds, the void that surrounds and permeates tension or pain, and even the space between the words on this page. And lastly, getting into nature and embracing its opulence, for nature is a direct reflection of the perfection, beauty, and love within you.

As I grow wiser and more in tune with Source, which I can only attribute to my years of meditation, I have extended the silence, the pause, the stillness, the deep breathing into ordinary moments throughout my day. It's a relief to give oneself to the present moment, periodically pausing and noticing colors, shapes, sounds, and smells while at work, performing mundane tasks, during leisure time, and even while in conversation. This is what I like to call mini meditation, which doesn't replace standard meditation rituals but may enhance inner calm throughout your day.

You may find welcoming the ordinary in this way is not unlike the benefits that come with a ten-minute walk in fresh air or inhaling pure oxygen. Oxygen bars tout improved focus, concentration, and memory. By the same token mini meditations can invigorate you and help you feel more alert without the cost or inconvenience. Sinking into ordinary moments as such reaps untapped treasures. As your mind instantly becomes clearer, you feel more vibrant, stress melts away, and you become more productive with less effort and complete tasks in less time. Profound ideas and solutions present themselves, and naturally your intuition becomes sharper.

What has meditation done for me, you ask? God only knows.

"God Is"

The air I breathe

The water that cleanses me

The food that sustains me

The space that surrounds me

The silence that stills me

And the emptiness that fills me

Chapter 13: Lost in Thought

"While you practice in this way, you leave behind everything that you now believe, and all the thoughts that you have made up. Properly speaking, this is the release from hell. Yet perceived through the ego's eyes, it is loss of identity and a descent into hell."

—*A Course in Miracles* (W-44.5:4-6)

Who is running your life? Are you? Or could it be that incessant, nagging little voice in your head urging you to do this, warning you against that—a torrent of fear tactics and manipulation all in your head. When we allow ourselves to be coerced by the inner critic, it saps our natural inclination to take responsibility for our life.

You can choose to listen to another voice. The voice of your inner Guide. This voice is fostered through the practice of meditation, as well as by embracing the present moment with steadfast awareness. You don't have to do as the small mind directs. There is another way. A way to break free. It starts by exposing and examining the incessant mind chatter. We are lost as long as we see no way out, no other choice. Thus far, we've brushed on emotion, alluding to the premise that emotions are the result of what we are thinking. This *is* the perfect time to take a closer look at the thoughts that form our beliefs.

Now that you've bolstered your intuition with practices that connect you to your inner light, you've begun forming a relationship with the voice of reason. The voice of love that never steers you wrongly.

The trouble is we mistakenly identify with the small voice. We identify with the small mind and believe it is the voice for good. It's pushy and loud and demeaning, and we've trained ourselves to either obey it or try to ignore it. Neither approach works for our highest good. Its job is to keep us stuck and living small. The inner critic produces wavering esteem and vacillating opinions—we are either the best or the worst and always wanting more. In this game we are mere puppets.

It is most important to identify these thoughts and examine them verbatim. It helps to write them down. Easier said than done, for thoughts travel through the mind at lightning speed in hopes of discouraging you from taking a hard look at them. Start with just one thought, the most charged one. After all it is just a thought passing through the sky of our minds, and a thought can be changed. As soon as you ask for help to see this differently, there is an opening. Ego is shaken loose. Challenge the validity of this thought, and the ego disengages because it is exposed for what it is. You can then change that original thought by rewording it to a more accurate, kinder thought. This is referred to as reframing.

"In silence, close your eyes upon the world that does not understand forgiveness, and seek sanctuary in the quiet place where thoughts are changed and false beliefs laid by."

—*A Course in Miracles* (W-126.10:1)

<u>Help Me See This Differently</u>

"Yet is salvation easily achieved, for anyone is free to change his mind, and all his thoughts change with it. Now the source of thought has shifted, for to change your mind means you have changed the source of all ideas you think or ever thought or yet will think."

—*A Course in Miracles* (W-132.2:1-2)

Joy is uncovered when we adjust our perceptions. "Help me see this differently" is the call we make for a change in perception, which is all that is needed to recover the happiness that we were meant to enjoy. Suffice it to say, when you are not fully joyful, a mindset adjustment is in order.

Get the past out of your eyes. Imagine for a moment how viewing things in a new light could easily replace frustration with understanding or discouragement with happy possibilities.

Happiness matters because it represents greater satisfaction in life, and it is linked with the potential to connect to the whole on a universal level. Yet it continues to elude us. In my exploration I discovered an often-quoted passage in one of the beloved stories in *The Big Book* of Alcoholics Anonymous that states that the key to happiness is acceptance. In and of itself, this is very freeing, and wouldn't you say it truly shifts the perspective toward a brighter outlook, a healthy step away from denial, and no longer fighting what is? Curiously, as I became more familiar with *A Course in Miracles*, I found the same phrase with one slight difference, which invites us to take happiness even further, stating the key to happiness is forgiveness.

Acceptance is a good starting place toward inner calm and contentment. We must accept ourselves and our circumstances before we can change them. But what if you could take it even further with one minor shift? Forgiveness is the key to happiness. This one step beyond the freedom acceptance yields heals our misperceptions at the core and thus opens a door to the oneness of love for all. Seeing past the lies that would control us ramps acceptance into sublime gifts of harmony in mind and spirit.

In the same vein, I've never been fond of the phrase, "It is what it is." Sure, at first glance, it rings of acquiescent acceptance, but to me, in that statement is a lingering hopelessness and sense of resignation. A giving up of sorts. What if it isn't what it is? What if it is a cloud of misperception? What if it is just a big imaginary billboard that blasts, "Give Up, Quit, Why Try!" Wouldn't you agree this tactic works beautifully to keep the collective stuck in a dismal, stagnate pool of apathy?

It's all too easy to nod our heads in agreement when we hear that phrase. Next time "It is what it is" crosses your mind or your lips, dare to dig deeper and consider it a golden opportunity to elevate your perspective. Say to yourself, "Maybe it isn't what I think it is after all." Ask for guidance from the Master within to see beyond, look past, and let go of your dreary notions. Somewhere, somehow, skirt past the low mind to the light and love toward the possibility of healing your heart instead.

Broaden your vision and look through what appears to be wrong until you can find a glint of what's right. Then zero in on that flicker until it expands into infinitude and beyond your former belief.

<u>Rise Above Soaring Eagle</u>

"If God's Will for you is complete peace and joy, unless you experience only this you must be refusing to acknowledge His Will."

—*A Course in Miracles* (T-8.IV.1:1)

I started out by asking for help while deeply experimenting with a workbook lesson in *A Course in Miracles* one entire afternoon. I made a concerted effort to let go of all my thoughts. Nothing more. Seems simple enough, but I found it took great concentration to catch my thoughts before they took me away in daydreams. At first, I questioned this practice, fearing that I might lose God's thoughts as well as ego's. A voice reminded me that letting go of a holy thought only expands and brings more of it, like releasing a butterfly only to have it linger longer.

Once identified, I envisioned the thought traveling from my center up a cord further and further, following it all the way through my mind's eye until it reached the apex of divinity and seemed to diffuse into the space of nothingness from whence it came. Then I waited for the next thought like a hawk intent on capturing its prey.

I am uncertain why it was so challenging. Perhaps this discipline was difficult because the lower mind is designed to lull us back to sleep, keeping us unconscious and unaware, and my nailing each thought as it arose was breaking a long-held habit of an undisciplined mind.

I cannot convey to you the profound peace beyond belief that overcame me after a few hours of this practice. For days I was living in a state of total tranquility, with no wants and absolute selfless acceptance.

Since then, I've only attempted this experiment in short spurts. It would be well worth dedicating another afternoon to revel in such bliss. I wonder what is stopping me?

Which brings me to a great question for you to pose to the voice in your head. Who is talking now? Whose voice is this? Is this the voice of my eternal Teacher or the ego's voice? These questions will stop us in our tracks every time. If you get an internal argument, it's the ego talking.

While facilitating, a participant often launches into an "ain't it awful" story, especially with regard to seeming ungodly world disasters, impending doom, or of how a dear friend or family member is suffering, and continues in rage and pity followed by a monologue of how somebody, usually the government, should do something. They slam their fist on the table, demanding that something must be done. Straightaway I am prompted from within to ask the above questions. All it takes is tuning into your higher mind to lift you above the limiting belief that life is unfair. As a soaring eagle rises above strong currents to new heights, we too have the means to rise above the storms of life.

No Problem?

"I think 99 times and find nothing. I stop thinking, swim in silence, and the truth comes to me."

—Albert Einstein

Scientists theorize that in this universe there is more empty space than form. The observable universe is more than 99 percent empty space.

Look at space, or in our case, our current chaos under a microscope, and what do you see? Nothing. Magnify one hundred times. Nothing. Magnify one thousand times. Still nothing. Magnify one million times. Absolutely nothing.

At this point, your higher Self would probably be satisfied and even at peace with the conclusion that the space that encompasses your current chaos is, in fact, nothing. This makes theoretical sense, and besides, in reality, we're beyond the world of form—in it but not of it. When we identify a problem and explore it more deeply we find there was nothing really there to begin with. This was yet another important lesson, revealing to us that our copious ego-devised troubles are but wild goose chases.

Just as when we see something from afar, it looks very different too. From a distance the soaring eagle has a purer perspective.

"From a Distance"

From a distance, the world looks blue and green
And the snow-capped mountains white
From a distance, the ocean meets the stream
And the eagle takes to flight
From a distance, there is harmony
And it echoes through the land

From a distance, we all have enough
And no one is in need
And there are no guns, no bombs, and no disease
No hungry mouths to feed

...

From a distance, we are instruments
Marching in a common band

Playing songs of hope
Playing songs of peace

. . .

From a distance, you look like my friend
Even though we are at war
From a distance, I just cannot comprehend
What all this fighting's for
From a distance, there is harmony
And it echoes through the land . . .

—Julie Gold, as sung by Bette Midler

This particular piece awakens an ancient memory within me. Without question the lyrics rouse higher vision. Both poetry and music awaken contented oneness and may act as a bridge to higher realms.

Examine closely the negative thought, experience the emotion, or explore the supposed imbalance further by taking a scope to your alleged problems. However, the lower mind isn't average. Armed with the fear of dissolution, the ego keeps on magnifying, gazing deeper and deeper into empty space until, out of nothing, ego suddenly conjures up yet another problem, tragedy to be fixed or a lofty goal to be achieved.

On the bright side, you have access to a power beyond your alleged problems. Not only is it your prerogative to change your mind, it's your calling. Dare to dig deeper and you'll find, like a microscope tightening in on an atom, that the supposed problem isn't even really there. It was merely empty space where the issue seemed to exist fueled only by your imagination.

Rise above, look through, see past the disturbances on earth that have kept you stuck, struggling, and stagnating. Not denying your pain, your perceptions, or your past, but diving into and through them to the other side. Peace bursts through the upset, and negativity dissolves into a wisp of ludicrousness leading back to unwavering certainty.

Look for the purity of Light! Sometimes it's hard to find the love and light that we are seeking amidst our problems. Is the world essentially good? In this world of so much to the contrary I found myself wondering if goodness really exists at all. In my quest, I have discovered that it depends on my perspective. How we see things is most definitely a choice. This is free will and a gift that we've all been given. The real questions are: Is the way you are looking at something the whole picture? Is your chosen point of view helping or hindering you?

In my experience gathering goodness simply means realizing it in the moment because, from a distance, the earth is alive with possibility, and so are you right now! We lose ourselves when we wallow in the countless woes in our lives, not to mention in the world, which dramatically dulls our happiness receptors. The beauty of perspective is you have the freedom to change it in an instant.

Navigating through the complexity of lower mind thoughts is the perfect segue into the next barrier, emotion. Very often emotions arise due to discursive, repetitive thought. Our tendency to hide our feelings or pretend we don't feel what we feel blocks spiritual progress. Self-denial is a lie to yourself and to God and undermines your true brilliance.

"Today we let no ego thoughts direct our words or actions. When such thoughts occur, we quietly step back and look at them, and then we let them go."

—*A Course in Miracles* (W-254.2:1-2)

Chapter 14: Riding the Rollercoaster

"Never approach the holy instant after you have tried to remove all fear and hatred from your mind. That is *its* function. Never attempt to overlook your guilt before you ask the Holy Spirit's help. That is *His* function. Your part is only to offer Him a little willingness to let Him remove all fear and hatred, and to be forgiven."

—*A Course in Miracles* (T-18.V.1:4-2:5)

The stories the lower mind continually runs set us up to rise to false heights and then come careening down.

Thought triggers emotion. When someone thinks the world is doomed as opposed to the world evolving, it elicits two very different feeling frequencies. Therefore, it is reasonable to assume if you could catch and reframe your thoughts in the first place it would make all the difference. And yes, that's true, as noted in the previous chapter.

Because thoughts fire through our brains so quickly, we are often incapable of pinpointing the thought before a flood of emotion comes crashing down through the gates. Once we become overwhelmed with emotion, I have found we will better serve ourselves by acknowledging, plunging into, and paddling through the current of emotion, lest we fall into the trap of suppressing or burying the emotion by trying to rationalize it away. This only adds more weight to a lifetime of this heavy bag of unprocessed emotion burdening us like a massive anchor that drags us down wherever we go.

The remarkable news is, with awareness, emotion can become a starting gate toward our healing journey, for as I have found, the only way out is through. If you've experienced trauma or major disappointments thus far, you can be sure your bag of unprocessed emotion is weighing you down. And like a riptide that pulls us away from safety, we experience overreactive behaviors and a flood of self-pity, interspersed with peculiar bouts of isolation.

After decades of stuffing our emotions it can frighten us to open the bag and look inside, but despite our trepidation, how else are we going to feel it in order to heal it? Feeling it is the beginning of healing it.

<u>Stay the Course</u>

"Our very being seems to change as we experience a thousand shifts in mood, and our emotions raise us high indeed, or dash us to the ground in hopelessness."

—*A Course in Miracles* (W-186.8:5)

Encouragement is golden. Most of us need plenty of it to walk through seemingly difficult inner work. It takes courage to walk through that which brings you pain.

It almost feels wrong to "sit" with uncomfortable emotions. A little like putting your hand to a hot flame. Nobody wants to feel lower-frequency emotions, such as apathy, anxiety, anguish, anger, or agony.

However, it is not by ignoring, pushing away, or running from emotions. The miracle ignites when you dive in with a spiritual teacher, coach, or guide until you can begin to access your inner Guide and field your emotions like a pro. This is true empowerment, and it's by coming out the other side that you find who you really are. You discover your authentic higher Self.

This process of permanently releasing emotion is so simple it would amaze you! I have found that overwhelming emotions don't arise to harm us—they arise to set us free. What could you do or be without the static of limiting beliefs or the flood of paralyzing emotion that surfaces as a result, not to mention the self-imposed obligation to do for everyone before yourself?

Fortunately, or some may say unfortunately, when an emotion arises and we embrace it instead of pushing it away, it not only releases the current emotion but gives way for deeper layers to release as well. By the way, as you'll see in the example later in this chapter, the process of releasing is effectively done within and not expressed outwardly toward another, as that may cause more damage and trigger feelings of guilt, suppression, and eventually an expression of it again in an unloving manner. This cycle is ego-driven and what we are asked to interrupt. In essence, every time you pause, identify, dive into, and let go of an emotion rather than lashing out at another, you are, in fact, venting the steam of past accumulated emotion.

I stress again that running away from surfacing emotion would be like hearing your name called announcing an all-expenses paid vacation to everlasting peace and freedom, but to rise from your seat, walk to the podium, and claim your winnings is too much work. Instead, you choose to decline your winnings and leave the auditorium. It doesn't have to be this difficult.

Yesterday, I laughed with a client so hard it hurt. Sharon had misplaced her credit card in my office and was for twenty minutes frantically looking for it, and, caught up in her frenzy, so was I. Finally we gave up and began her session by meditating deeply into the moment. As she did so, the panic dissolved like a lump of sugar in a cup of hot tea. Upon our last cleansing breath, she immediately started fussing with the pillow she was sitting on and pulled her credit card out from under the pillow. You should have seen the expression on her face! Here was proof that diving into the moment and letting go of overwhelming emotion works every time, for the feelings of panic very effectively had blocked Sharon's clarity and intuition.

Get Real

The little group that I facilitated agreed to do an at-home experiment for two weeks. Twelve like-minded souls dedicated to the concepts of *A Course in Miracles* eagerly received this instruction. We were to sit in front of a mirror, look into our own eyes, and repeat the words "I love and approve of myself," an affirmation recommended by iconic author Louise Hay.

With paper and pen at our side we jotted down each feeling as it arose. Reportedly, some of us actually noticed love, joy, and peace, but after a few rounds, that which was hidden began to surface. As instructed we simply observed the feeling with curiosity for several seconds. Most admitted after a few more rounds, they felt disgust, sadness, and other lower-frequency emotions that seemed to come out of nowhere. As they continued, apprehension, rage, and resistance arose even to their own reflection. Despite the uneasiness, they followed through with the experiment.

With each emotion that came up we allowed ourselves to sink fully into the sensations and vibrations, then repeat the affirmation again. Could we be imagining or perhaps conjuring up these emotions? I suppose it is possible. However, if you are feeling it, it is most likely old suppressed emotion, and you are enriching your quality of life, as I have discovered by purposefully cleaning house.

Authenticity is achieved when we can allow ourselves to feel exactly what we do. This willingness acts to shed light, and in that moment the upset is transformed. The good, the bad, and the ugly. What we bring to the light becomes the light! It's not by denying it but by embracing all that seems to arise that you find the direct route to your higher Self.

When the group returned, all who'd given themselves to this simple practice were astounded at the peace they found in the act of observing emotion within with nonjudgmental curiosity for just five minutes a day. When you identify the emotion, you're being honest with yourself, and while giving it your full attention, it is transformed into your natural state of tranquility—one emotion at a time.

You cannot let go of what you won't admit is there. Imagine trying to declutter your home without digging through the closets first. You have to pick up the article of clothing, decide if it is worth keeping, and if not, put it in the trash or in the give-away pile. You see, pretending like you feel and think everything is okay does nothing to heal your heart. In truth it just burdens you further by adding to your heavy bag of repressed emotion.

Emotions as well as thoughts are just passing through. They aren't who you are. They do not define you. Identifying, exploring, and letting them go clears the logjam of buried emotion. And as noted, the same goes for thoughts. A negative thought must first be identified and then examined for its validity. Only then can you reframe the thought and let it go. Once we become willing to see it differently, Spirit swoops in to shine a light, exposing a kinder thought that helps rather than hinders. Suddenly it becomes easy to reframe it. Ignoring, including outright denial of a negative thought, only increases its hold on you.

"I am never upset for the reason I think because I am constantly trying to justify my thoughts. I am constantly trying to make them true."

—*A Course in Miracles* (W-51.5:2-3)

A Curious Observation

After practicing the mirror exercise with my ACIM group for a while I noticed a pattern. As you may recall we were to jot down each emotion as it came up while looking into our eyes, fully experiencing it. A definite pattern began to emerge. The same emotions, almost in the same order, played out—bliss, sadness, frustration, anxiety, peace, acceptance—and back again, like a merry-go-round. However, with each pass the intensity usually lessened as it resurfaced.

This made me ponder the books I'd read that pointed out how the world isn't doing it to us. Rather, we draw certain experiences into our lives to have yet another opportunity to feel and heal our misperceptions until all residue has dissolved and only peace remains. We free ourselves in this manner to experience real joy and peace unclouded by the clutter of rejected and neglected emotion.

In other words, situations are responded to or reacted to very differently due to our personal triggers, not because of the specifics of the situation but because of the hidden emotions calling for release within us. Have you ever noticed how two individuals' responses to the same stimuli can vary from complete indifference to total overreaction?

Just as the lessons in *A Course in Miracles* are actually affirmations, I have found any affirmation becomes more potent and more real for me when I allow for my initial doubt, resistance, and feelings of disbelief. This is accomplished by giving myself full permission to pause and acknowledge my visceral reactions to the words while repeating them. That is all that is required for the Holy Spirit to transform that rush of doubt and disbelief into undeniable certainty, authentic joy, and peace.

This morning when I awoke, a wave, more like a tidal wave of sadness and grief, flooded over me. I gave myself to it, the tears, heaviness, a raw and gaping inner wound, clutching vulnerability—a helpless sense of victimization. I did my best to attend to this energy, noticing it mostly in my chest and gut. To my relief, my steadfast conscious presence acted to release the overwhelm after a quarter of an hour or so. Nothing preceded this flood of deep sadness except perhaps the recent loss of my dog. The shock of losing her so abruptly probably set me up to put aside most of my grief. This, too, shall pass, and though a bit sensitive now, it is passing, and I can honor the residue of sensitivity. This is true "higher-self" care. We learn to trust the process of emotion and its necessary cleansing properties. On some level, peace and joy lie beneath all surfacing emotion!

There is a world of freedom in no longer pretending. A world of freedom in realizing who you really are, knowing your carefree, childlike essence. A world of freedom in exposing and refusing to believe the stifling rush of lies concocted by the lower mind.

"You who are steadfastly devoted to misery must first recognize that you are miserable and not happy."

—*A Course in Miracles* (T-14.II.1:2)

Chapter 15: Prison or Passageway

"The body is merely part of your experience in the physical world. Its abilities can be and frequently are overevaluated."

—*A Course in Miracles* (T-2.IV.3:8-9)

Thus far we've discussed the deluge of big emotions that seem to throw us off balance and the whirlwind of thoughts that form our beliefs that then rule our actions, both of which divert us from our natural state of peace and consequently impact our physical existence, not to mention our health and wellness. The main character in this saga is our physical body, including health, chronic busyness, and all we must do to navigate the world of form. We are not our body, but it is through the body in this realm that we can access peace. Moreover, our body can act as a conduit to extend love and light. The body does not last, and what does not last is not real. It is not who we are because who we are is beyond the physical world. If the body isn't who we are but a product of ego, then why should we make it the focal point of our existence on earth? Yet, we spend years, not to mention time and money, shaping it, hating it, idolizing it, trying to heal it, demanding too much from it.

The body can be idolized, appeasing it with a multitude of delights one after the other, while on the other hand, the body can seem like a prison of sorts and is, in reality, but a meager vehicle. It is not our source, but it is easily mistaken for who we are. After all, it appears that we are inside this body, and all that it seems to experience is but a reflection of this mistaken identity. The only way to correct our perceptions is to undo our beliefs about it and simply go along for the ride by observing all that the body seems to experience. No, it is not by denying it, masking the symptoms, or obsessing over it.

"The ego uses the body for attack, for pleasure and for pride. The insanity of this perception makes it a fearful one indeed. The Holy Spirit sees the body only as a means of communication, and because communicating is sharing it becomes communion."

—*A Course in Miracles* (T-6.V-A.5:3-5)

Body attacks, Spirit extends. In this way, Spirit can use everything toward love and healing this body to which we have allowed ourselves to become so attached. Just like diving into thoughts and emotions, diving deep into whatever the body is experiencing can be a segue to inner peace. When we experience pleasant sensations, we will enjoy them more deeply if we stay in the moment and let go of the manic desire to have them continue forever. And when we successfully let go, we experience more of the peace that we are, for it is our clinging to these temporary, pleasant sensations that throws us off track and leads us into the loop of desire—wanting more, always—insatiably wanting more. This state only takes us further away from our ultimate goal of freedom, bliss, and serenity.

You may know someone who can't get enough extreme sensation, the masochist who seems to wish for more pain or drama, or the proverbial adrenaline junky. It makes them feel alive. Why is that? It can be seen for them as a means of temporary escape from the dullness or stress of their inner narrative, for both risk-taking and drama act to stimulate endorphins.

Some revere the body, while others see it as an impossible ball and chain unable to keep up with its needs. A demanding, unquenchable volcano that must be appeased. Beating yourself up mentally and physically until you rebel and throw in the towel. This loop keeps us hating ourselves, stuck, sick, and tired. On the other hand, there are those terrified of injury or illness and take great pains to avoid discomfort. The body's inevitable aging, illness, and fragility may sooner or later catch our attention. And yes, it calls for maintenance like any vehicle. Problems arise when we try to make it into something more than a temporary residence. When we're younger it seems to bounce back no matter how we might abuse it. Of course filling it with noxious elements, for instance alcohol, drugs, and excessive sugar, pushes it beyond all limits and exposes it to roads it wasn't built for, like taking a Porsche up the side of a steep, rocky, deeply rutted jeep trail still expecting it to perform.

As the body ages a natural condition of the world of form occurs, and just like a flower or a mountain, all things decay and eventually return to dust. Our vehicle can no longer take the hits to which it has become accustomed. Identification with the body leads us to conclude we're getting old, yet we are trapped in appeasing it at all costs, including escaping into destructive habits. The body cannot help but fail us again because it is only dust in the wind. Even if we take excellent care of it, we can do everything right and still land in the hospital for one unanticipated reason or another. We are sentenced to this body until it eventually fails. Turns out the joke is on us because the dust, a product of ego, was never there to begin with.

The lesson then becomes an opening that acts as a passageway to higher wisdom and leads us through the illusion of form, back to the peace and bliss we were seeking all along. Ironically this can be achieved through the body.

To best utilize the earth suit that you seem to inhabit: Appreciate it for what it is and provide it with whole foods, pure water, fresh air, sunshine, quality sleep, and enjoyable movement. We need not make our bodies the focus or take perfect care of it, which would only further glorify it. However, when it is maintained, as you would a vehicle, and relieved of imbalance, it becomes less of a distraction and more of a conduit for channeling love.

I received a letter from a former client, Jan, a few months after she had completed the Higher Self Care Holistic Wellness Program, in which she had changed the course of her life and, consequently, dropped eleven pounds.

"It was mid-July when we first began our journey together, and little did I know what a fabulous journey it would be for me. As I walked into your office, I had some parameters that I wanted to work within. Firstly, I wanted someone who could hand me the answers to my problems. Secondly, I wanted someone who could supply me with these answers and in short order. And lastly, I wanted it at an extremely reasonable cost to me. I wish I could remember what you said on that day, but it seems like you only said a few sentences and apparently the "right" few sentences because I knew at that exact moment that I was in the right place. I knew that I was led there, that I was supposed to be there, and that I was not there by accident. Even at the expense of throwing all my pre-planned parameters out the window.

Prior to our beginnings, I was aware of a feeling that I was an empty box, a shell. I had no thoughts of my own. I did not even know who I was, as I had lost my own identity. I was a robot that made a list of things to do and worked my list every single day of my life for at least twelve to fifteen years and perhaps even longer. I was living a mere existence, stuck in stagnation and misery, and could not find joy or happiness in anything outside of myself to help me.

As we began, my issues were about my dad and how they affected me. I felt that I was somewhat limited on how much I could grow because I had to do everything under the pretense of how it would impact my dad. You worked very gingerly with me as you continued to ask questions, poking and prodding me all along the way. We made headway every week in basically working through what I would call my original wounding. As time went on, with a lot of water that went under the bridge for dad and me, you and I finally moved out of the dad segment and transitioned to the next step, Jan's new life. It was as if I wanted help for myself, but I had to work through the original wounding before I could grow and finally focus on myself. I can now look at the bumpy road and see what a beautiful process it was.

Prior to the wellness coaching program, I was the sole spectator of my life. I watched my life happen to and around me, and ever more so, I took on a victim role, as I had no control. I have now become a full participant in my life. I can listen to my inner voice and Higher Self first . . . and then I can make better choices. I rejoice that I have become an active player in the outcome of my continuing journey.

I have learned that I am worthy and loved unconditionally. I live my life more consciously, more mindfully for me. I would say I live it more heart-fully and gut-fully, as this is where I feel my answers first. I eat more intuitively and exercise more consciously. I have a better sense of life's balance and awareness, and I wake up happy every day, with joy in my heart, and I enjoy it all day long no matter what happens.

As we continued through this journey, I visualized an onion as each layer peeled off. Now I can visualize a rose, going from a bud and blossoming into a full rose . . . and I owe it all to this program.

When I started this journey, I never once looked back. You helped and supported me every inch, every step of the way. You have given me the tools and the confidence to continue to blossom. In fact, I can honestly say that you were 'Universe Sent.'

Thank you from the bottom of my heart. Love, Jan"

This kind of support begins with asking for divine guidance. During this opening you are gently led to pause and breathe slowly into the moment, which instantly disengages us from egoic notions. When you plug into your inner Guide, I gently ask you to jot down the direction that comes to you. While in this state of communion with Source, divine ideas come through even though they may not seem to make sense. With this the body becomes a passageway through which sacred wisdom flows. After I guide you through the initial confusion, I ask if you could choose just one idea that seems the most exciting, brilliant, or doable. Oddly, in that moment you know exactly which action to take, no matter how minute. It will be sound and clear. It is never wrong because you can be certain it came directly from the divine. We meet again in a week or two and observe together how this one action step played out.

Often by taking this leap of faith, clients are inspired to do more. They not only fortify their intuition by coming up with the next step in collaboration with their higher Self, but saying it out loud to another keeps them more accountable.

The act of writing does the same thing. We retain as much as 75 percent more when we write it down, so we're more likely to follow through. The client may take it even further by putting this action step on their calendar and for the next two weeks implement this direction as best they can. Successfully letting go of the results for now, they are often surprised and delighted to notice when the date is up on the calendar that more of the imbalance has dissolved. That is how we excel in earth school. Each assignment completed teaches us that all our answers are found within.

Simply slowing down, looking past and beyond the body to the timeless beauty within, results in childlike inspiration and humility. The recipe to freedom starts with pausing long enough to ask for help.

In the same way, rebalancing the physical includes the busyness. Chronic busyness that many experience in this time of "faster is better" and "instantly is supreme" is epidemic. Life imbalance is bound to happen with so much to do, so much to take care of, so many demands. The striving and driving on our earth walk is instigated by none other than the small mind which incidentally feeds off of the imbalances we experience.

For example, your spirituality seems balanced but your career is lacking, or your finances are good but your relationships are troubling. So many areas of your earth walk can draw you away from the truth of who you are, the peace within. Why can't all these areas just stay in balance? The good news is imbalances can also be utilized by Spirit to bring you back to center. Instead of procrastinating, your job is to courageously identify the area that seems to require attention and, with curiosity, explore it further.

The Brilliance of Breath

"You can use your body best to help you enlarge your perception so you can achieve real vision, of which the physical eye is incapable. Learning to do this is the body's only true usefulness."

—*A Course in Miracles* (T-1.VII.2:4-5)

A breath of fresh air. A time-tested way to utilize the body for higher vision is through the breath. The breath has long been known for its transformative qualities, for within the practice of following the breath Spirit is found.

In the case of pain, we surrender to it instead of trying to escape from it while, of course, following your health professionals' advice. Take a magnifying glass to it, so to speak, to observe it, see it, and feel it—at a molecular level—going deeper and deeper in your mind's eye. Suddenly the pain has lessened or completely dissolved. Our willingness to take a closer look has broken the spell of falsity wide open. It may be brief, but I assure you this shift is no illusion. At its core pain results from resistance and non-forgiveness as well as the belief that you are somehow guilty and thus deserve punishment.

Check inside. Locate a place of tension in your body or perhaps pain, perhaps a nagging inconvenience that is always there but you've done your best to ignore or forget. Pause, breathe, locate its central point to the head of a pin and notice with each breath the dullness, throbbing, pulsating, or pinching sensations. Breathe into it slowly with full awareness. This may cause anxiety or even nauseate you. Dare to dive deeper into every sensation in this moment. You may have a visual of this. Continue to observe all that you experience as best you can. Notice after a minute or two during this process that something has shifted and maybe lightened up a bit. You've successfully gone beyond the body by diving into and through perceived discomfort utilizing only your breath.

Pain is common while inhabiting bodies, yet it offers an opportunity to come into the moment. Again, always consult your healthcare professional for the proper remedies or treatment. Once that is taken care of, I have found our instinctive inclination is to avoid pain. Yet, it is a bridge to divine intervention. At the molecular level pain is just energy after all. Much of the discomfort we experience occurs because we are trying to get away from it. If possible, let go of any resistance to it. If you are unable to let go of the instinct to push it away, then surrender to the sensation of resistance. Escape the world you see. Detach, coming into the now into your body, and inhale and exhale deep long breaths. The inner strife will naturally melt away.

"Of one thing you were sure: Of all the many causes you perceived as bringing pain and suffering to you, your guilt was not among them."

—*A Course in Miracles* (T-27.VII.7:4)

It's an art to consciously pause and sink into the body. This simple practice elevates you directly into the moment, which, by the way, is the only point in time you will access your higher Self. Follow the breath, and you will find your true essence. Your physical prison will then become your passageway to peace.

Part III: Undoing the Madness

Chapter 16: The Only Way Out

"How is the peace of God retained, once it is found? Returning anger, in whatever form, will drop the heavy curtain once again, and the belief that peace cannot exist will certainly return."

—*A Course in Miracles* (M-20.4:1-2)

Inner wisdom, universal love, Great Spirit wants to heal all unease, and it can only do that if we give our troubles to Source. Once we identify and let go of our deepest feelings and beliefs, a sense of relief occurs, and in rushes the miracle of enlightenment. Walking through what disturbs us is the way out.

Pretending that you're fine when you are not is common in this world. We have been programmed to dismiss anything that seems the slightest bit negative and deny feelings of depression. We have grown to fear our thoughts and feelings—afraid that if we take a good look at them they will get bigger. We never permit ourselves to truly experience our feelings because they may take us over, and we may never come out of the abyss of lower-frequency emotions such as sorrow, anxiety, or hatred. I've known many who will not allow themselves to feel the hatred that is welling up within them. They tell me that they hate the word hate and refuse to say it, let alone admit that they may be experiencing it. This only keeps us stuck in hate.

The difference between sleeping and waking in this world correlates precisely with unconsciously allowing ourselves to be carried away into the many distractions the small mind inundates us with, not unlike the proverbial frog in a pot of slowly boiling water. On the other side of the spectrum, mindfulness can act to open the eyes you never knew you had beyond the body and give you the courage to dive into upset, knowing that the only way out is through. The light of awareness shines negativity, overwhelm, and imbalance away.

Why not just slather your problems with positive thinking? One of the pitfalls of relying solely on positive thinking is that it keeps us apart from the now, separated from our experience. We continue to pretend. We have lost ourselves by denying what we are feeling or thinking. We forget that we are much more than a bleak thought floating by or the undertow of deep sadness.

Don't get me wrong. Repeating positive affirmations can be a powerful practice, but be aware that if it is a falsehood, as some part of us knows it's a lie, it won't sink in no matter how many times you repeat it.

As noted previously, one sure way to sync an affirmation is to give yourself full permission to really tune into what you feel when you recite it, then let the emotion dissolve and continue to repeat, rinse, and repeat until little charge remains. The affirmation will either start to come alive inside you, or you will be moved to tweak it until it rings true or discard it altogether.

More on the Pitfalls of Positive Thinking

"We are lost in mists of shifting dreams and fearful thoughts, our eyes shut tight against the light; our minds engaged in worshiping what is not there."

—*A Course in Miracles* (W-192.7:4)

What is positive thinking anyway? Positive thinking is a mental attitude in which you expect favorable results. In my experience it is difficult to keep this up all the time. We are bound to let our guard down, and negative thoughts come swooping into our heads courtesy of the lower mind. It's the nature of this ego-dominated delusionary realm that we think we inhabit where no one is immune to the inner critic.

Anything that insults you or another is not your inner wisdom talking. On the other hand, true intuition is heard as a soft voice or gentle urging often emerging from your gut or heart. Using outside means, such as positive thinking, to stave off the doldrums doesn't work in the long run. Does this shed some light on our use of sugar, alcohol, caffeine, and other easy-to-obtain mood-altering substances? Yes, in excess they are all futile attempts at boosting dopamine to hopefully douse negativity. Martha Graham, a choreographer named "Dancer of the Century," explains inner wisdom best.

> "There is a vitality, a life force, a quickening that is translated through you into action, and there is only one of you in all time, this expression is unique, and if you

> block it, it will never exist through any other medium; and be lost. The world will not have it. It is not your business to determine how good it is, not how it compares with other expression. It is your business to keep it yours clearly and directly, to keep the channel open. You do not even have to believe in yourself or your work. You have to keep open and aware directly to the urges that motivate you. Keep the channel open. No artist is pleased. There is no satisfaction whatever at any time. There is only a queer, divine dissatisfaction, a blessed unrest that keeps us marching and makes us more alive than the others."

Sure, positive affirming can be helpful, but not if it's used as a smokescreen to cover up a plethora of old beliefs that no longer serve. Most certainly you will end up overwhelmed by limiting thoughts again. In my experience, positive thinking without taking a deeper look at your underlying thoughts and feelings may actually interfere with higher healing and growth. The truth is positive self-talk may pull us away from our intuition and keep us stuck.

Recently, Laura, a client, shared a podcast she'd listened to that encouraged her to repeat a positive mantra. She repeated the beautiful mantra-like affirmation over and over again. She describes what she discovered.

> "I didn't truly believe what I was saying. The words were just words, almost mechanical in nature. On top of that, despite the beautiful words, I couldn't ignore

the fact that the unworthiness, doubt, shame, inadequacy, and remorse that I was trying to push out of my head were just growing stronger. I wondered, if I had time to repeat it one thousand times more, would it finally begin to sink in and deliver the positivity I was seeking?"

Who knows if that would have worked for Laura. Nevertheless, she couldn't ignore the snowballing agitation in spite of this uplifting affirmation that she was reciting ad nauseam.

When Laura realized it was having the opposite effect, she got honest and acknowledged the unwelcome emotions. In that moment she allowed herself to experience these lower vibrations. After less than two minutes they completely lifted, and, to Laura's surprise, her beautiful affirmation came alive within her. She reports, *"I felt a surge of strength and inspiration that seeped into my very cells."*

Repeating positive affirmations can be a clever way for the ego to keep you whistling in the dark. What is blocking your capacity to experience real joy? I urge you to uncover it and let the light of conscious attention shine it away. Self-love sometimes requires the rigorous honesty of dispelling untruths so your eternal brilliance can radiate from the inside out. Real transformation cannot occur until we address our personal barriers. Is it time to get honest?

In the pages that follow, I extend to you proven accounts, gentle guidance, and encouragement.

What Lasts Forever?

"All that is not rooted in love is coming to the surface to be healed."

—Author Unknown

The fact is, on the other side of diving in and through your problems, there is only love. But is it safe to love?

It's the perfect time now to realign with your highest purpose. In this world it's easy to get sidetracked, for tragedy, disappointment, and injustice seem to dominate the media and hijack well-meaning thoughts, causing us to become skeptical.

What is real love? In this world of so much to the contrary we can only wonder if love exists at all. What's your definition of love? Not so much romantic love, which would be a whole other subject, but the all too elusive unconditional love.

Some describe it as affection without any limitations or love without conditions that can only be sourced from within. You may feel it as you watch a falling star, catch it emanating from a toddler, or receive the unmistakable look of total love from your pet. Definitions vary, but most experts will agree that unconditional love is that type of love that is limitless and unchanging.

The key word for me is unchanging. In a world of change, what can we possibly experience that never changes? This is a great question to ask yourself when you realize that true security lies in the changeless. I have pondered, "What never dies and lasts forever? What does not separate? What does not judge? What is kind to all? What dispels prejudice?" And oddly, I can only come up with one answer—unconditional love.

Having lost loved ones, I've proven to myself beyond a doubt that the love we shared never dies. As mentioned earlier, I can still recall the memory of love given and received and hold it in my heart as if it never left. And no one and nothing can take that love away. From a broader perspective we are the essence of love and are capable of extending that which never dies, even beyond death.

Love is abundant, limitless, and forever within us because it *is* us. When we focus myopically on the atrocities that we see almost every day it only serves to pull us further into despair and apathy. Taken on faith, through the body's eyes and ears, that this is just how it is. This attitude of resignation heals nothing.

Does merely extending love in these situations mean we're doing nothing in spite of perceived discord? Hardly. When we are rooted in love we are more connected to our higher Self, free and guided from within to do what we can to help, knowing that to allow ourselves the dubious luxury of repetitive thoughts like "ain't it awful" hinders our beneficent voyage back home.

By focusing on love we are effectively expanding our vision to encompass the reality of a universal experience of total oneness. I'm not suggesting that we suppress our emotions. However, harboring hate, wanting to force change, or languishing in sadness only make seeming injustice more glaring, which pulls us further away from the ever-present but easily overlooked universal power of love.

Is this a silly idea or a powerful mindset shift? Ancient wisdom repeatedly advises to look for love in situations even when we're convinced it is nowhere to be found. Worldwide spiritual teachings focus beyond bodies, beyond time and space, to the love that is here within you and me now. Is that so mystifying?

Those of you who apply this new frame of reference will find delicious changes in your thought patterns, drawing in real joy, peace, and liberation. With divine assistance you have the power to get out of your current state of mind by sifting through and releasing the opinionated notions that would seem to keep you in hell. This practice serves to motivate you further because you are no longer hopelessly trapped in the whirlwind of dispirited "doom and gloom" rationale. You can pull love up in a heartbeat, certain this kind of healing power knows no limits.

Chapter 17: The Rabbit Hole

"It is the other part of your mind that functions in the world and obeys the world's laws. It is this part that is constantly distracted, disorganized and highly uncertain."

—*A Course in Miracles* (W-49.1:3-4)

Alice's tumble down the rabbit hole begins as a wildly frightening excursion that transports her deeper and deeper, where she ends up some place beyond her old world in a strange and wonderfully surreal land.

Down the rabbit hole, or in this case down, through, and out the rabbit hole of old beliefs, overwhelming emotion and physical concerns with conscious attention are filled with new ways of seeing and bring you back to center, freer with less baggage each time. Emerging from the rabbit hole with a renewed love for life and newfound innocence, lit with clearer, unclouded vision, is a wonderful and strange opportunity to hone intuitive fortitude.

Today in mid-meditation my old habits of overdoing and overgiving led me down the rabbit hole into all the ways I could help or fix a client who was on the brink of a major breakthrough, all while in the midst of navigating some tough issues. My thinking splintered into how she could do this or that, if I said the right thing, or suggested the right exercise with her, I could make her way easier. Thankfully, I became aware of wanting to fix another and asked Spirit to help me see this differently, to see her beyond my limited perception that she was afflicted and needed my help to get past this to the perfection that shines beyond thought. I let go of the intrusive need to fix it and allowed Spirit to empathize through me. I went back to seeing her in truth—perfect, whole, and complete beyond my thwarted delusions of grandeur. And as is usually the case, in the next session she experienced a cathartic breakthrough without me needing to fix anything. Imagine that!

As pessimistic as it sounds in my description of this ego-dominated chaotic world of never-ending ups and downs, to reiterate, it is really about how quickly you come back to center. You see the distractions that continually pull us away on earth—a memory, a story, an upset, including problems and tasks such as feeding the kids, making sure the bills are paid, and trying to manage your weight, fitness, or rocky relationships—all of which are incidental, or shall I say instrumental, in reminding us to come back to center.

For example, heart rate recovery (HRR), a medical term for how quickly your heart returns to normal after you stop exercising, is determined using your heart rate at the end of your workout. This calculation is a measure of your physical fitness and an indication of your heart health. How can we then improve our rate of spiritual recovery? By regularly accessing the place where intuition is found—the Source within.

Just as cardiovascular health is determined by how quickly after strenuous exercise your heartbeat returns to its resting rate, the same goes for the frantic beating off the path we experience while navigating earth lessons, which act as a pop quiz, if you will, to see how swiftly we emerge from the rabbit hole. How quickly we return to our natural inner calm can be an indicator of spiritual fitness. The mark of spiritual wellness isn't avoiding the ups and downs that pull you off-center, for this is just another inner growth assignment to complete. Spiritual wellness is more about recognizing that you are off center and how expediently you return to center. In this world we're not going to eliminate the rabbit holes.

"It is the belief conditions change, emotions alternate because of causes you cannot control, you did not make, and you can never change."

—*A Course in Miracles* (W-167.4:2)

Check inside. Are you feeling alone, upset, or discordant right now? Your emotional state is an accurate indicator to determine if you have once again tumbled down the rabbit hole.

Black and White

"The term 'right-mindedness' is properly used as the correction for 'wrong-mindedness,' and applies to the state of mind that induces accurate perception."

—*A Course in Miracles* (T-3.IV.4:3)

As mentioned earlier, everything in this realm is under the law of duality. While navigating the world of form we seem to see that everything has two sides. Everything has a pair, and everything seems to have an opposite.

The term duality may designate the character of two elements of differing nature. This is unlike nondualism, which emphasizes unity amidst contrasts and, to me, the element of universality and our true natural state of oneness that exists in an eternal continuum beyond the tangible differences we think we see. Yes, in this world what goes up must come down. Even the sages are continually seeking center.

The insanity is kept alive by the whims of the small self. We have distinct halves in the realm of form—the higher mind and the lower mind. The lower mind controls you through a barrage of recycled stories, all based on fear of the future and fueled by the regrets and injustices that linger from the past. We mistakenly believe that we are these thoughts, and furthermore, we allow these untruths to define us. And so we identify with them to such a point they literally direct our every move on earth.

"Never confuse right- and wrong-mindedness. Responding to any form of error with anything except a desire to heal is an expression of this confusion."

—*A Course in Miracles* (T-2.V-A.13:1-2)

Spirit simplifies and ego complicates. The small self's inner monologue locks us in by constantly convincing us that "we can't, it's not fair, we shouldn't, we have to, and do this or else," thus causing us to be short with others, impatient, and even demanding. We're hearing in our head that either we're just not good enough or we're better than others.

Sometimes we surround ourselves with people who vocalize their dissatisfaction, but I've found when you take presumably a healthy step by removing yourself from these ill-willed individuals in hopes of outgrowing the ego, then these stories don't necessarily die but remain now circulating in your head. For instance, you have, for the most part, overcome the emotional trauma, but when the stakes are high you hear this dreadful dialogue looping in your head like background noise.

No, life lessons aren't going to stop occurring, but that's the fascinating part: seeing how quickly we become aware of the chaos and return back to the breath, back to "asking for and accepting help from a power greater than ourselves," back to center. An exercise geared toward improving our spiritual fitness.

The calm center is just that. Blissful, carefree, childlike, in the moment, trusting, creative, effortless, also known as nirvana—a state of transcendence in which there is no suffering, desire, or sense of self, immersed in the universal flow of love, a holy perpetual timeless instant of total oneness. Can you imagine the boundless ecstasy that comes with no sense of a separate self?

The art of coming back to center is as simple as coming into the now, for this very instant is your access point. This is precisely how we transcend our misery from the inside out. Transcendence means literally to climb beyond. When you achieve transcendence, you have gone beyond the ordinary limitations of the world of form. I've found the most favorable method for achieving this is to become conscious of the sensations in and around your body and environment. Then, make the decision to ask for help from your inner Guide. This may be as uncomplicated as uttering the words "Please help me." Decision is your superpower while in this realm.

"Decision cannot be difficult. This is obvious, if you realize that you must already have decided not to be wholly joyous if that is how you feel. Therefore, the first step in the undoing is to recognize that you actively decided wrongly, but can as actively decide otherwise."

—*A Course in Miracles* (T-5.VII.6:1-3)

The more you ask for help, the help to decide to see things differently or to have the willingness to see things differently, the more these instances string together. At that one point in time is the real world of eternal peace revealed to you and you are free. You have been transported into a wonderfully serene state of mind. You are perfect peace. Eureka! Herein lies the key to opening the door to the peace beyond belief. And isn't now the only time that matters in the whole of reality?

Examine with courage and curiosity the thoughts you are thinking. This act sheds light and a truer thought emerges. Experience it by diving into the emotions that are surfacing now. Allow yourself to freefall deeper down the rabbit hole and leave all judgment behind. Your willingness will let the emotions diffuse into the ethers and transform back into the perfect peace that you are.

The curriculum is quite literally that which stirs the past beliefs that upset us. The assignments are to dive into the rabbit hole of upset, and the means is the willingness to ask for help to complete the homework, homework being the inner work. The willingness to make another choice.

Healing opportunities come in many forms, but they are always occurring here and now, in the body, the breath, the pain. A problem arises. What, you say you have no problem? Wait for a short while, and one will surface soon enough. The problem arises with resistance naturally, which is your alarm going off, reminding you it is time to ask for help. Then, dive into the assignment by sinking into whatever you're experiencing right now via bodily discomfort, repetitive negative thoughts, or emotional overwhelm. Your cue is when pain, pressure, or upsets occur.

"I almost wish I hadn't gone down that rabbit hole—and yet—and yet—it's rather curious, you know, this sort of life!"

—Lewis Carroll, *The Adventures of Alice in Wonderland*

Chapter 18: Into Fear or Into Flow

"If you raise what fear conceals to clear-cut unequivocal predominance, fear becomes meaningless. You have denied its power to conceal love, which was its only purpose. The veil that you have drawn across the face of love has disappeared."

—*A Course in Miracles* (T-12.I.9:9-11)

Is your desire for control controlling you? Trying to manipulate people, situations, and things indicates a lack of trust and serves only to keep us apart from our Creator. This ever-present Source of love naturally flows to swiftly dislodge the logjams in what would otherwise be a babbling brook of contentment.

Fearing an objectionable outcome, do you feel the need to aggressively control your life, your circumstances, or the lives of others? Losing yourself in the lunacy of trying to control people, places, and things will sweep you into the eddies of wrong-minded thinking.

The best way to let go of this all-consuming need for control is to give up your desire for control. Surrendering control elicits spiritual alignment, all while eliminating the heavy load of self-imposed stress. Surrendering control is a decision that will reconnect you to an unceasing current of omnipotent strength that is available to each and every one of us.

Wanting Control Stems From Fear

After Dwayne and I purchased our home, I tortured myself and him for months by wanting control of everything being done the way I wanted it in the house. You can imagine how this taxed our relationship and smothered feelings of spontaneity and warmth. My unresolved fears stemmed from the need to believe I was in control of something, anything, just to feel safe—an unfortunate flashback from the instability I endured as a little girl. However, this coping mechanism to force some sense of order was no longer working for me and was mercilessly usurping the harmony in our home.

With the desire to resolve this and bring sanity back into my life, I chose to take one baby step at a time, which started with one day a week of committing to go with the flow in our home. And things began to change for the better. On occasion I catch myself falling back into those antiquated behaviors, but thankfully I am reminded from within to pause, ask for help, and humbly find my center once again.

Wanting to change things outside of yourself is an exercise in futility bent on wearing you out emotionally and physically. Have you ever been successful at truly changing another individual? Observe yourself the next time you are in the grips of wanting control over situations or someone else, such as your parents, children, spouse, or coworkers. Check in with yourself and notice how tense and unsettled you become.

The bottom line is we cannot control much in life—especially others—and it is with the relinquishment of control that we begin to really live in the gracious flow of joy and peace. Wanting control can appear as rigid non-acceptance of people, places, and things. For instance, wanting to "help" someone without being asked, wanting to fix things that are in the past, or wanting to change circumstances that are obviously out of your control.

This pattern can wreak havoc on what otherwise might be healthy relationships, not to mention your peace of mind, squashing joy like an overripe grape. Love cannot exist in the midst of control.

Let's break down wanting control versus living from your center. Wanting control is the opposite of having control because the more we want control, the more out of control we become. Wanting control is actually just another emotion originating from fear, the polar opposite of surrendering to divine flow. Wanting control leaves no room for divine guidance. It chokes out our natural inclination to lean into our higher, all-knowing self.

All this time I thought my desire to interfere, especially with regard to my family and friends, was based on love. UNTRUE. When you take a moment to really look at wanting control, it is based on fear.

"Fear has made everything you think you see. All separation, all distinctions, and the multitude of

differences you believe make up the world. They are not there. Love's enemy has made them up. Yet love can have no enemy, and so they have no cause, no being and no consequence. They can be valued, but remain unreal."

—*A Course in Miracles* (W-130.4:1-6)

In today's fear-based society, many people experience frustration, anxiety, overwhelm, or loss of enjoyment. Too much information leads to anxiety from trying to change everything, from themselves to their family, neighbors, and colleagues. There's too much going on, too much worriment, and we cope by clinging to controlling behaviors. Unfortunately these behaviors rob us of joy and the opportunity to experience harmonious interconnection with ourselves and those whom we value.

Manipulative or controlling tactics do not allow for flow. On the contrary they are the barrier to the universal vibration of ease. Synchronistic universal flow occurs when we surrender to what is happening, becoming an aware and unbiased observer. Trust is knowing that all is well no matter what arises. Inner flow happens in the now. Learning to trust the all-knowing Source appears with the choice to plug in, and you often don't realize the selfless inner calm that is present until after you've experienced it. You have been fully present with yourself and others without trying. In that instant you are a shining conduit as a copper wire harnesses the power of electricity, allowing divine light to pulse through. There is nothing more satisfying.

My obsession with wanting to understand why—why did this happen, why didn't that go the way it should—has also kept me stuck just as effectively as wanting to fix it, or wanting security, or wanting to be liked. When I finally began to let go of my need to control people or potential outcomes, it provided an opening that helped me to realize our oneness on a level beyond illusion. Ego's mode of operation is "wanting to figure it out" and is precisely what keeps us stuck. We empower ourselves once we dare to go beyond the small mind and take that intuitive leap. We begin to trust what we cannot see with the body's eyes. Now we are fully committed to put to test the wisdom of something greater than ourselves.

Awareness Is the Key

What could you do or be without the static of limiting beliefs or the flood of paralyzing emotions that surface as a result, not to mention the assumed obligation to fix everything and everyone? We'd like to say fear is the culprit here, but it is in actuality the bridge. It is only by becoming aware of the fear that we are able to grow beyond these limiting thoughts and emotions. "Fear" goes by many names, from mild trepidation to heart-stopping terror. Acknowledging fear is actually a catalyst to freedom. Until we identify and allow ourselves to experience this emotion we cannot let it go.

Denial, as stressed previously, is costly—and to pretend that we aren't afraid comes out sideways, such as wanting control—

and actually works against us, which drives us deeper into hopelessness and serves only to keep us stuck.

Fear has many guises, as we'll uncover in the following chapter.

Chapter 19: Playing With Fire

"Anger takes many forms, but it cannot long deceive those who will learn that love brings no guilt at all, and what brings guilt cannot be love and *must* be anger. All anger is nothing more than an attempt to make someone feel guilty."

—*A Course in Miracles* (T-15.VII.10:2-3)

Forgive your long list of grievances. They are judgments based on the fear that you can be hurt and only serve to tighten the chains binding you to the lower mind and its bizarre belief system. What is anger really? On some level it is another aspect of wanting control.

"Don't play with me 'cause you're playing with fire." I related to these Rolling Stones lyrics in the seventies, especially when licking my wounds after I stood by while someone, usually a potential boyfriend, would flirt with another or in some other way treat me disrespectfully.

Anger, resentment, and acts of revenge backfire like splattering oil in a hot skillet and burn us every time. Each of us experiences low emotions, but we've loosened their hold on us when we've identified and acknowledged them with honesty.

To act on these impulses, such as trying to get even, fighting back, or sticking it to the man, is the ego's way that keeps us locked into a downward spiral that spins into the abyss of nowhere. If we are all one beyond the body, to hurt another is synonymous with hurting yourself. You cannot harm someone intentionally without harming yourself. That would be as ridiculous as deciding to drink poison with the expectation the person you resent will get sick. In my case, my petty, childish fights with significant others played out just like that every time. Trying to make someone suffer the sting of regret or guilt will only make you feel worse in the long run.

Fear, sadness, and anger are just passing through, so it is crucial to your peace of mind to own them with awareness and let them go. It can only impede your journey toward enlightenment to allow yourself to be ruled by squelched emotions. When you admit, acknowledge, and release them as they come up, it will foster real peace and oneness with all.

Often when I give myself permission to witness these lower-frequency emotions it results in less confusion, and many times, as the emotions dissolve, I experience crystal clarity. I then realize that I don't have to address it by confronting the other, as just releasing it was all that was needed. Alternatively I get a download on how to compassionately discuss the issue, letting go of the inner charge and my attachment to the outcome.

Case in point, for the first year Dwayne and I were married, we didn't have one disagreement. It was smooth sailing until that second year when we began quarreling. He'd verbally strike out at me and I'd withhold affection. Then tension would build up in me and I'd lower the boom on him. He would retreat into a world of books or leave me alone at home for hours as a result. A very unhealthy passive-aggressive cycle, to be sure. As we grew out of this deleterious pattern I began noticing that when he opted to slam the door and stomp out angrily that he'd come home with a dent in his truck or once he came home with a traffic ticket. On the other hand, after I'd be cold, responding with cruel and cutting remarks toward him, I would internalize it and almost immediately get ill, experience an asthma attack, or suffer from insomnia until it got resolved. And like a boomerang that hits you in the face, we were both hurting ourselves by trying to even the score.

Remember the childhood riposte, "I'm rubber, you're glue"? The cruel things you say to me do not stick to me. I do not let them hurt me. In fact, the insults you have thrown at me will bounce off of me because I am rubber and impervious to your slurs. However, you are glue. What you have said to me will bounce off me and stick to you.

Furthermore, what you say about me really says more about you. The unkind things you choose to say about me are most probably a reflection of how you have judged within and what you suspect unconsciously to be true about yourself. I'm rubber. You're glue. What you say to me bounces off of me and sticks to you! Attack brings attack on yourself.

I concur with Edwin Markham's sentiments in his "Outwitted" poem.

> He drew a circle that shut me out—
> Heretic, rebel, a thing to flout.
> But Love and I had the wit to win:
> We drew a circle that took him in!

Nothing anyone does maliciously or due to ignorance or knee-jerk trauma reaction can hurt us. The "us" beyond the body. In the same vein we cannot really hurt one another. Attack only harms the attacker, whether in thought or action. This doesn't mean we stuff our feelings of fury. As noted earlier, emotions are best honored and then surrendered to Holy Spirit to be transformed back into love and light.

"Shut off from your Self, which remains aware of Its likeness to Its Creator, your Self seems to sleep, while the part of your mind that weaves illusions in its sleep appears to be awake. Can all this arise from holding grievances? Oh, yes! For he who holds grievances denies he was created by love, and his Creator has become fearful to him in his dream of hate. Who can dream of hatred and not fear God?"

—*A Course in Miracles* (W-68.2:1-5)

When we experience hate, anger, or vengeance it follows that we believe we can be hurt and are therefore unsafe, putting us constantly on edge, which often results in anxiety, apprehension, and paranoia. Our unresolved grievances directly correlate with our underlying feelings of shame and inadequacy. Why not cease collecting grievances? Why not give up the role of victimhood? You have the power to make a different choice.

I'm not free until I reconcile the thoughts that tell me I have been wronged, taken advantage of, or mistreated. In this next segment I share a couple of instances of how I have freed myself from the bondage of victimization.

That Noisy Hallway

I lease a beautiful space on the second floor of a building with about sixteen offices of various sizes. The architect designed it with frosted glass windows in every office as well as skylights to allow the natural light, as exterior windows were only in the outer few offices. The designers elegantly furnished it with chandeliers along the cathedral ceilings throughout the building. My office was perfect for all the services I offer, with a corner for the equipment needed for bioenergetic testing, including a small closet to store remedies and enough room to accommodate small meetings and private sessions. I had two tables custom-made just to fit in my oddly shaped but perfect space.

Today, I couldn't be happier with the amicable atmosphere in our building, but it wasn't always this way. Unfortunately, even with my door closed, sound vibrations traveled from the hallways and adjacent offices due to all of the glass, as windows are one of the most common sources of exterior noise incursion. I discovered that if an adjacent office closed their door the sound would be dramatically muffled and tolerable enough for me to maintain my concentration on work tasks. Needless to say, over the years I've had to remind tenants to keep conversation to a minimum in the hallway and to please close their door when having conversations. To complicate matters the rooms could become stuffy with the doors closed, and everyone liked to have their doors open, including me.

A new business popped up in the building, a young startup business that held four or five employees in an office space meant for one. As you can guess, they were busy, loud, and solely focused on growing their business. I spent the next year or more asking them to please shut the door when conversing to no avail. They would close it, sometimes loudly, when I asked, then seemed to forget my request. After some time I brought this to the attention of the landlord. Nothing changed. I felt like a victim, as if they were out to get me.

Finally, after losing much peace of mind and productivity I decided to give it to God. One night I earnestly asked Source to solve this issue, and yes, I may have pleaded, begged, and demanded to the universe previously but never so sincerely and humbly as on this occasion. In that second I completely turned it over to God. Interestingly, with this request, I immediately noticed myself shift from hate and resentment to understanding and compassion. I drifted to sleep that night with a calm I hadn't felt in a long while.

The very next day I arrived at work and saw a moving van on the street and the hallway lined with boxes. It seems the little startup company had grown so much that they were able to relocate to a bigger space! I almost fell over in shock at the fact that I'd asked for help with this, and it was resolved the very next day.

Here I am again with the same issue but magnified. A few months earlier I'd seriously considered relocating to a wellness center in the city, but after months of deliberation I decided to stay put. In the meantime a young attorney rented space in our building, and his business began flourishing over the next couple of years. His team now occupied all of the offices adjacent to mine and across the hall.

Throughout the day they would have interoffice conferences with their doors wide open. It only caused dissension for me to request that they close their doors when having meetings. I taped up a sign in the hallway to remind them to close doors when holding meetings, which was seen as petulant on my part and taken down. I talked to the landlord again and was told that things change, and if I wanted to, I could break my lease. I'm sure I was expendable as the attorney would have no trouble acquiring my office as well. Little by little, despite long-standing tenancy, I became the minority.

Yesterday I did the same practice where I gave it to God fully and completely. Something told me there would be a solution in the morning, and with that, I finally fell asleep. The next day I opened my course workbook to Lesson 23:

"I can escape from the world I see by giving up attack thoughts."

"The idea for today contains the only way out of fear that will ever succeed. Nothing else will work; everything else is meaningless. But this way cannot fail. Every thought you have makes up some segment of the world you see.... If the cause of the world you see is attack thoughts, you must learn that it is these thoughts which you do not want.... There is no point in trying to change the world. It is incapable of change because it is merely an effect. But there is indeed a point in changing your thoughts about the world. Here you are changing the cause. The effect will change automatically."

—*A Course in Miracles* (W-23.1:1–2:7)

I began giving up my attack thoughts at every annoyance, though things didn't seem to change overnight. I felt better and smiled more. Everyone seemed much friendlier, and eventually my work environment improved. Was it me that changed, divine alchemy, or was it a coincidental natural occurrence?

"How glad are we to have our sanity restored to us, and to remember that we all are one."

—*A Course in Miracles* (W-241.2:3)

The Embers of Addiction

Speaking of fire, there are numerous substances in this realm that can reduce our soul to ashes due to their habit-forming properties. The chemical responses in our brains are wired to repeat pleasurable activities, forming compulsive, out-of-control behaviors. Furthermore, with the need to resist pain of any kind, coupled with the innate longing to experience bliss in this world of separation, we're bound to come across addiction, whether we experience it ourselves or witness it in a friend or loved one.

It seems addiction is rampant and recovery a rare miracle. This has grieved my heart with regard to loved ones, as addiction appears to rob them of innocence, potential, and sensibility. Addiction is the result of wanting to soothe away or avoid past pain or feelings of guilt. A compulsive clinging to "feeling good" when emotional distress surfaces has its price. The substances or activities, after repeated use, become the problem. In essence the issues you were trying to smother aren't the issues anymore, as the addiction has taken on a life of its own and becomes impossible to control or halt without divine intervention.

If I could change the world, I would eliminate addiction to mood-altering substances, prescribed, legal, or illegal, for they each take away the potential for lasting happiness in my mind. Isn't addiction a desperate attempt to find God in the world of form, an idol, a quick fix? I know in my case it was. It periodically continues to grieve me heavily due to losing loved ones. The loss of connection with another dampens my soul as I believe they are slipping away into oblivion, gone forever. It's the one thing that deeply grieves me in this world and how it has impacted me and others in my life—lost love, hope, and passion, as well as deep sorrow for loved ones who seem unreachable, including premature death. In the throes of grief I am reminded that I cannot change or control anyone and choose instead to see them beyond my perceptions of illness and doom.

But even this is a road back to center, right? Some souls, mine included, need a story that consumes and brings deep despair to them and to all who love them. They need to experience true powerlessness. This is the ego's bottomless pit. And yet it is at the bottom of the rabbit hole where we find the miracle, a radical change of mind. The light shines through the tiniest honesty, delivering a miracle that can only be found in that inescapable corner of your mind where you've no place else to go. This is where even addictive personalities can find a power greater than themselves and begin the first step on the road to recovery. For me, wrestling with the belief that I can lose family members, cherished friends, and husbands not through death but addiction effectively hijacks my sanity.

Still prone to bouts of heartache, I stay sane only by tapping into higher vision, which allows me to see beyond my perceptions to the love and light that they are in truth—to envision them instead on their unique journey to God. The principles of Al-Anon are very helpful to realign my thinking.

The ego has its hooks in me. After I've banged my head up against the wall, trying to change things or to help them in some way, and when I finally have had enough anguish regarding the suffering of another, I remember God's love. A universe of love pours through me with a mere request. I remember in that moment that if I'm upset it's because I believe we can be hurt. It is at this point I am moved to ask Source to help me see this differently beyond my limited perception, to help me see beyond the body's eyes to the beauty, wholeness, and perfection that links all living things. And with that meager request I know healing light and love have been received at the highest level.

"Now we go in peace to freer air and gentler climate, where it is not hard to see the gifts we gave were saved for us."

—*A Course in Miracles* (S-3.II.3:4)

Chapter 20: The Trappings of the Small Mind

"The ego can and does allow you to regard yourself as supercilious, unbelieving, 'lighthearted,' distant, emotionally shallow, callous, uninvolved and even desperate, but not really afraid. Minimizing fear, but not its undoing, is the ego's constant effort, and is indeed a skill at which it is very ingenious."

—*A Course in Miracles* (T-11.V.9:1-2)

Wants. The small self, the inner critic, the ego convinces us we are always lacking. It is part of our split mind. It uses fear to control us. Absolutes that put pressure on us, such as should, shouldn't, must, and have to, and extremes, such as never, always, and doomed, declare inescapable outcomes. These definitive words serve the ego well. Waging war in the name of God and then blaming God for the aftermath.

It keeps us down and dissatisfied and then projects our misery and discontent onto the people around us, coworkers, friends, and family, transfixing trusted authority figures into enemies. It doles out just the right amount of mistrust mixed with the promise of hopeful outcomes. A chorus of thoughts made to imprison thirsty souls. It is cunning, pervasive, and ever-stalking.

Wants ensnare us with promises of independence and freedom while dangling the carrot of superiority. Its greatest fear is dissolution because it knows it is nothing, an erroneous idea, a mistaken belief, so it must keep our attention. The all-important small self wants to keep us in the dark. When we pause, we shed light on it and can only then see how ludicrous these untruths really are. It builds the past into a future that cannot be escaped.

When we hurt badly enough we do something that ego fears greatly: We cease listening to the chatter in our heads and look beyond it to the still voice of Spirit. When we admit complete defeat in the darkness and plead to something greater than ourselves, ego is extinguished like a candle in the wind because it was never really there to begin with, as it was only our attachment to its senseless droning that kept the embers of its falsehoods stoked. It is, in reality, nothing.

The small mind keeps us just a misery short of looking for God. As long as we believe in this nonsense it will continue to cause us pain and misery, and we will remain imprisoned in an endless maze of lies.

The world of duality, as we've discussed, imposes opposites such as up and down, black and white, good and bad, right and wrong. The right Mind knows at an intuitive level and moves you to gentle action versus the wrong mind or ego, which in order to exist it must believe it knows all, but being nothing, it cannot know. From this frenzied ignorance the small mind forces often harsh manipulations to "make it happen," regardless of who, what, and how it destroys. Paradoxically, in truth it can destroy nothing that was not real in the first place.

Ego is a liar, no matter the name it goes by—inner critic, friend, advisor, common sense, conscience, saboteur. It constantly keeps us on edge like a con artist lurking in the shadows taunting, "Do this and you will be free," or promising if you achieve that self-centered goal, especially at the expense of others, you'll always be protected, favored, and prosperous.

The lower mind cajoles us into taking everything personally. Ergo, we must be right, even at the cost of happiness. Paranoia prevails. This is your cue to rise above, look through, and see past your experiences on earth that have kept you stuck and struggling. Again, it is not by denying your pain, perceptions, or past but by diving into and through them to the other side.

> "You must have noticed an outstanding characteristic of every end that the ego has accepted as its own. When you have achieved it, it has not satisfied you. This is why the ego is forced to shift ceaselessly from one goal to another, so that you will continue to hope it can yet offer you something."
>
> —*A Course in Miracles* (T-8.VIII.2:5-7)

Goals not divinely inspired are ego driven—another myth that keeps us locked in chains. When you reach the goal, the glory is fleeting, so the small self pressures you to find another goal. You are trapped in the downward spiral of the ego's rabbit hole of distraction. It is indeed lonely at the illusory top, which effectively boxes you out of the realization of your sacred oneness with all life.

How many times have you lost the weight, made the money, landed the job, attained the fitness, and then its appeal wore off only to be replaced with another goal? Somehow it keeps us just this side of satisfaction, forever trapped in the loop of perpetual desire. This has never been more apparent than in intimate relationships. For instance, after the honeymoon phase has faded you see your small self as yoked, bound to this person that you've chosen to spend your life with, but behind closed doors their inadequacies show up. Their ugliness, which is really a reflection of the mistaken beliefs about yourself, is projected outwardly onto your beloved.

Interpersonal communications become skewed. You can't see clearly in the darkness that ego blindfolds you, so your mate becomes your enemy. Devotion is not tolerated by ego, and you find one thing after another that doesn't suit you or that you absolutely abhor. You spend weeks that morph into years, putting them down openly or inwardly mumbling their faults to yourself. You are locked into trying to change them because, from the perspective of the wrong mind, they just don't measure up. You find that according to the small self you were mistaken about them. You may begin to question your commitment.

If ego is not criticizing you, it is trying to convince you that it's your duty to whip this person into shape and pressure them or manipulate them based solely on your ego-driven fears. If you were to look at yourself squarely in the spotlight you'd

THE TRAPPINGS OF THE SMALL MIND

realize that you are the one who needs to change, at least change your mind, which is death to the ego.

In this physical world, we cannot escape the ego's sway, but we can coax it from the shadows. You can be certain that the many hurts that you've kept alive will surely leach into your relationships. The ego persuades me to keep rolling the stories from my past and rehash this inner narrative—the incessant small-mind chatter that elicits shame, guilt, and unworthiness—including the story of how I believed I was mistreated and abused over and over again. This only added to my heavy bag of self-pity owing to feeling justified in extruding retaliation onto others. Oh, woe is me. This rehashing begins to define me and control my actions, moods, and health. I spend days in despair, anger, and remorse and nights lying in bed trying to figure it all out, overwrought with anxiety and worry, and cannot stop the cycle no matter how hard I try.

The ego's sweet spot. It has got you and me right where it wants us.

"You will be bound till all the world is seen by you as blessed, and everyone made free of your mistakes and honored as he is."

—*A Course in Miracles* (W-200.5:3)

The ego looks for what is wrong, sees the worst, and triggers suspicion where delusions and hallucinations haunt our minds, causing us to become terrified, jumpy, and potentially psychotic. We are not in touch with reality. Is this not bordering on mental illness or what some would call spiritual dis-ease? Is there no hope of escape?

As soon as you recognize and become aware of upset, discontent, or unworthiness, apart from trying to fix it, you're on your way to dissolving the influence of the lower mind. As you may recall, trying to fix it is a contrivance of the ego. The ego's game of diversion. This realization is the impetus for change. A change of mind. Is it possible to disengage from the demands of the imaginary world of ego?

It begins with humility. A.A. reveals the first step toward freedom: Admit that we are powerless and that our lives have become unmanageable. ACIM reminds us that in this realm we do not perceive our own best interests. Presently, although we reside in a body and are bound by ego, we have been given the power of choice and can yield to superior wisdom upon demand.

"Those who remember always that they know nothing, and who have become willing to learn everything, will learn it. But whenever they trust themselves, they will not learn. They have destroyed their motivation for learning by thinking they already know. Think not you understand anything until you pass the test of perfect peace, for peace and understanding go together and never can be found alone."

—*A Course in Miracles* (T-14.XI.12:1-4)

May my words remind you how insignificant the small mind is and, on the downside, if unchecked, can rule every aspect of your trek on earth. It will continue to pose as a rescuer, a cheerleader, or a bully, depending on its one goal, which is to keep us separate, competing against each other and as far away from love as possible. As we see it for what it is, it becomes easier to bypass.

Ego fades as we gain the humility needed to strengthen our relationship with an unerring realm, a power greater than ourselves, our higher Self. Of our small self we can do nothing. Until we are privy to the trappings of the small mind we cannot experience the peace beyond belief.

"Would you be hostage to the ego or host to God?"

—*A Course in Miracles* (T-11.II.7:1)

Chapter 21: Dust in the Wind

"The distractions of the ego may seem to interfere with your learning, but the ego has no power to distract you unless you give it the power to do so. The ego's voice is an hallucination."

—*A Course in Miracles* (T-8.I.2:1-2)

That brings us to that million-dollar question. How do we dissolve the ego?

The ego is really just dust in the wind. However, ego in its arsenal uses words. Words become weapons, such as "evil," for example. This is a useful concept, aiding the ego's fear tactics in an attempt to goad us into denying responsibility for our mistakes and stuff any guilt by projecting it onto an external agent, thus coming back to frighten us with its "evil." As mentioned before, instilling fear is an excellent strategy for controlling the masses.

Nancy, my original *A Course in Miracles* facilitator encouraged us to replace the words evil, devil, and Satan with ego. It takes the power and fear out of the "evil" when seeing it for what it is—ego—which is really nothing. These are the words that instill terror that would support the ego's constant threat. Do this or else.

Ego abhors the concepts of humility, unity, love, forgiveness, charity, freedom, joy, and peace, for it must keep you separated, in want, and believing you need no one. On the other hand, it is not above using these very words to pull at your heartstrings to manipulate you.

Hard times get so hard that if you're lucky you'll experience a spiritual awakening that breaks through the egoic thought system. It only takes one holy instant. Go deep. It's okay, it's safe, and it's time. Notice the moments out of time when intuition is calling from within to foster spiritual reflection.

Gina is noticing a shift from bold action since bolstering her alignment with the divine over the past few weeks toward feeling more introspective, easygoing, and spiritual. Like a calming wave lulling her to slumber, she feels as if she's being swept into deep thoughts and emotions. She finds herself moving more gracefully, dancing while doing chores, and if her husband would join her she'd dance with him too.

The divine is calling each of us, urging us to tap into our creative side and to tune into the wisdom within, aligning with sharper intuition and wondrous creative imagination.

Although Gina is aware of a constant tug to do, act, and force things, it seems strife has taken a temporary back seat. She begins to ease herself into the calm. She trusts the inner still voice and immerses herself more deeply. She has discovered allowing the mind to wander into soundless stillness is a necessary condition to achieve true serenity and spiritual connectedness.

This dip into the void is nature's way of reminding you to pause and experience the bliss that can only come with the miracle of surrender. It's not only safe but paramount to go inside, slow down, relax, and reflect.

As Gina ponders her goals, dreams, and desires, there is a mystical air that surrounds and permeates her being with contentment in the moment and a profound glow of gratitude bathing her in the tranquility of starlight. She notices more compassion, understanding, and forgiveness toward others, and others seem more thoughtful toward her too. Even her sleeping dreams seem more mystical and prophetic.

It goes without saying when we align with celestial currents we naturally become more receptive and empathetic. And with your feet planted in the corporeal you shall occasionally get whisked away by sorrow, misunderstood, or lost in the clouds of lower thought. The answer is to bring that mystical air into all that you do with the awareness of a sentinel.

And when you do get pulled away from your center—and you will—is this so bad? Maybe so, maybe not. We learn from all experiences in life. Awareness is key because, after all, this is earth school. How do you allow yourself to embrace that which you cannot see, touch, taste, or smell? How do you keep your feet in this world while dancing with the divine?

Somehow slowing down in the moment seems easier lately. It never ceases to amaze me how I let my lower driving and striving thoughts control me. What a gift to realize joy is found in the moment just as it is. As you breathe, feel, touch, hear, smell, and taste the world around you, you discover an inner calm that was forgotten in the constant busyness.

Hearing Voices?

Which voice do you follow? Lester Levenson, the inspiration for the Sedona Method (an easy-to-use, practical guide to releasing emotional tension and one of the cornerstones of my practice) used to say, "Intuition is only right one hundred percent of the time."

Succinctly speaking, there are two voices in our heads. The small self and the higher Self. The question is how do we weed out the small self? The first step is getting good at deciphering the two voices.

Recognizing the wrong mind is surprisingly uncomplicated. This is the voice that induces fear, panic, anger, and greed. It's frantic and causes tightening and distress in the physical body. This is the voice that incessantly insists there is something wrong with you or another. It's unreasonable, pushy, and cunning. This is the voice that urges you toward impulsive actions and persuades you to forget the consequences.

Our real higher Self is never nagging or manipulative. You'll know it as still and soft. It often shows up when you slow down and soften into the present moment. It can only come from within, like a quickening or inner urging. It is characterized by an almost other-worldly knowing, which at the time may make no sense, yet you are compelled from within to follow the gentle guidance.

Once you've given yourself permission to slow down, pause, and tune in to your inner Teacher, confirmation to follow your intuition will pop out like colors on a painting that are vibrant and clear. And upon that choice, ego's ranting will only be a blurred and faded memory. The small mind chatter slips away and you feel lighter and gain a certitude that was only muffled before.

Are you scratching your head wondering if the road to eternal peace could really be that simple and direct? Here's your chance to test it out. Pause throughout the day with the eagerness of a fine-nosed Labrador to identify which voice is trying to coerce you and which is tenderly leading you.

You can raise your vibration in every way simply by slowing down and tuning within. You will naturally become more authentic and aligned and awaken the unblemished direction, creative purpose, and universal love in which you are immersed.

Go ahead and tune into your inner narrative. Who knows what you'll discover, for this is truly your way through the small mind's fog of confusion, second guessing, and madness.

"Do you really believe you can plan for your safety and joy better than He can? You need be neither careful nor careless; you need merely cast your cares upon Him because He careth for you."

—*A Course in Miracles* (T-5.VII.1:3-4)

Chapter 22: Your Best Interest

"For they are all but aspects of the plan to change your dreams of fear to happy dreams, from which you waken easily to knowledge. Put yourself not in charge of this, for you cannot distinguish between advance and retreat. Some of your greatest advances you have judged as failures, and some of your deepest retreats you have evaluated as success."

—*A Course in Miracles* (T-18.V.1:4-6)

I've completed *A Course in Miracles* lessons twenty-plus times in my study groups and several times on my own over the course of four decades. I highly recommend studying the content of this cutting-edge, far-reaching spiritual philosophy in a group setting, if possible the first time around, whether with an online or in-person group. Please keep in mind *A Course in Miracles*, albeit a very direct route, is one of many universal paths to enlightenment.

During my focused approach to reading the text, doing the lessons, and studying the teacher's manual, I would not stray far from the concepts of this spiritual philosophy. Something inside told me this was my answer. I kept it always nearby, especially while meditating, and would randomly flip open the book, asking for the content on the pages to reveal to me what I most needed to hear at the time. For well over seven months it would consistently fall open to a specific lesson: Lesson 24.

"I do not perceive my own best interests."

—*A Course in Miracles* (W-24)

As you might imagine this would frustrate and confuse me. I'd think to myself, "Of course I know my own best interests. Look at how long I've dedicated my life to spiritual growth." This weird occurrence set in motion a cascade of lingering doubts that would trickle in, causing me to feel tempted to toss the book aside.

I remember one year when I was studying with a group in Carbondale, how, as was the custom, we would privately focus on the same daily lessons and meet weekly in person to discuss shifts in perception, share our experiences, or ask any questions that arose. Oddly, I would see these individuals randomly in passing or while running errands in the distance during our mutual commitment to this group study. Ironically, although most of the participants had been acquaintances for many years, we'd not seen each other for countless months prior to studying these concepts together. Sometimes we would do our best to meditate at the same time each morning, which I believe strengthened our connection by leagues, not only to each other but to all on some level.

Often the participants would claim that their lesson was perfect for whatever occurred that day. Coincidence? On one particular day our lesson was Lesson 153 (ACIM, W-153).

"In my defenselessness my safety lies."

As usual I took the lesson to heart and repeated it frequently throughout the day. It happened to be my day off of work, and I could hardly wait to get outdoors, so I slipped on my boots and took off up a hiking trail that led to Mushroom Rock. However, this time I went deep into the wilderness, further than I'd ever ventured, when I stopped dead in my tracks. A very loud ominous growl and then a second more vicious gnarl rendered me motionless. It seemed to originate from the woods just beyond the clearing directly in front of me, not thirty feet from where I stood. The hair on the back of my neck stood on end, and my heart almost stopped. Adrenaline shot through my body like a bullet, with visions of a crazed mama bear or territorial mountain lion.

My mind flashed to *The Far Side* cartoon I'd found amusing the day before, which depicted a dead hiker with two large bears standing over him rummaging through his backpack looking for granola bars. This only escalated my terror. Instinctively I did an immediate about-face without lifting my eyes or making any sudden moves, shuffling my body back down that mountain as quickly as I could. The lesson for the day was repeated several dozen times under my breath on my descent. As I neared the bottom of the trail I could see the fresh footprints of a large beast that had overtaken and periodically crisscrossed my path.

When I shared my adventure with the group we laughed hysterically. Yes, indeed, in my defenselessness, my safety lies. The point of this lesson, at least for me, is what we defend against we make real and are prone to magnify larger than life. I will never forget the literal benefits of defenselessness, for defenselessness is a strength because it recognizes the awesome power of your higher Self within.

"Yet is defensiveness a double threat. For it attests to weakness, and sets up a system of defense that cannot work. Now are the weak still further undermined, for there is treachery without and still a greater treachery within."

—*A Course in Miracles* (W-153.2:3-5)

Meandering back to my original story... The pages would fall open to the same lesson, and this continued to happen regularly regardless of which *A Course In Miracles* book I picked up. It could have been any of the three that I own or even one from the shelf at a bookstore or library that I'd leaf through. Yet there it was again: "You do not perceive your own best interests." Very flummoxing, owing to the fact that I was posing serious questions in hopes of finding the perfect words to provide direction. Was it saying that I don't know what's good for me? What was the message I wasn't getting but needed to hear?

Finally, after wrestling with this for the better part of a year, it hit me over the head like a club. Without acquiescing to our inner Teacher, in all honesty there is no way I can know what is best for me, for of myself what can I know truly? Now when I see that lesson and choose to humble myself and ask Great

Spirit to decide for me, I always secure peace-enhancing direction.

By the same token, you have the power to connect with others beyond the physical, right here, right now, simply by envisioning your oneness with them in your mind. I promise that on the level of the right mind they will receive your light because this is not imagination but, in truth, very real. This is reinforced all the time when I extend love to others in this way, far or near, and they later tell me that they recognized this somehow. One time, while away at college, my granddaughter pulled out a unique rock that I'd given her just when I was envisioning her as perfect light. Another time, at the precise moment of extending light, my son told me later that he'd been looking up at the stars pondering his life.

Richard Bach authored a touching book, *There is No Such Place as Far Away*, a children's book with a profound message for all. My precious niece Janae lost her mother, my little sister Jackie, when she was only five years young. She would travel a thousand miles by plane alone to Colorado for summer visits, and we couldn't wait to reread this book together. The story, filled with breathtaking illustrations, instilled within each of us a mutual understanding that no matter how far away she was we would always be connected. This timeless mystical wink is just as certain for loved ones who have discontinued their earth walk as it is for those who reside afar.

Funny how when I practice envisioning another's light beyond the seeming shadows of so-called evil and gloom I am rewarded with a warm wash of unspeakable peace like a soft, regenerative waterfall flowing through my whole being. For myself this is all the validation that my soul requires to convince me that my gift has been received.

All lessons on our earth walk distill down to the actuality that we are all one, we cannot be hurt, we are perfectly innocent just as we are, infallible and immortal light-beings, and our inner Guide holds our hand every step of the way back home no matter the detours we may encounter.

To challenge your curiosity, I extend to you who have read this far a personal invitation. I meditate every day at Mountain Standard Time between six a.m. and seven a.m. What if the universe wants to connect us on this ethereal level? From my experience, Spirit knows we are already eternally joined in love, and it longs for us to recall this ancient knowing so we might fully realize our sacred oneness. Source gently offers us unceasing opportunities to learn lessons toward this end.

Let's explore together. Practice five or forty-five minutes of silent meditation between the hours that I do wherever you may be on the planet. I will most definitely recognize our oneness, and I promise your higher Self will too. We shall both realize that we are one with all life in that instant, which expands beyond time itself.

"There is no veil the Love of God in us together cannot lift."

—*A Course in Miracles* (T-16.IV.13:9)

Chapter 23: If It's Not One Thing

"But having accepted the errors as yours, do not keep them. Give them over quickly to the Holy Spirit to be undone completely, so that all their effects will vanish from your mind and from the Sonship as a whole."

—*A Course in Miracles* (T-7.VIII.5:5-6)

Get used to filtering by acknowledging emotions, thoughts, and mindless mistakes as they present, and you'll need to do it less. You will stop reacting and simply respond by asking for help to see things differently. This saves precious time and prevents more misery. That is what realizing the peace beyond belief truly encapsulates. Have no doubt ego will provide plenty of grist for the mill, so to speak.

My husband, Dwayne, and I argue less these days. Instead of opting to blame, think the worst, and find fault, we are more likely to let things roll off our backs. We're more apt to look inside for the answer or, better yet, laugh about it. Dwayne has gotten in the wonderful habit of saying "do-overs" in the midst of a heated exchange or a day that started off on the wrong note—a daring and courageous act of humility that lets a comical flicker of light into our petty disagreements.

As I'm writing this we've had an explosive exchange, both wanting to be right . . . over what Dwayne promised was on a menu that wasn't, which disappointed me. After almost losing an entire day over such a trivial thing in battle, both silent and vocal, we awoke the next morning with a hug and a chuckle, and after a couple of apologies everything seemed better again.

As we reflected on this Dwayne admitted there was a point, a distinct moment, where it flashed through his mind that he could have chosen to respond differently, but clinging to his pride, as we so often do, he brushed it away. Interestingly, my response to his brash words was initially calm, but later the story gained momentum in my head of "being treated unfairly," which continued to grow in intensity. I then became cold and distant when I could have easily let it go and instead decided to wage a counterattack. Spellbinding, isn't it, when you can see that we both became acutely aware of an instant where we could have chosen to respond with understanding? It looked as if we were bent on retelling an old joke that wasn't funny anymore, somehow expecting it to bring the house down today.

Some days we excel at earth school, some days we revert back to old ways. Every communication is a choice. Will I opt for right-mindedness this time or wrong-mindedness? From the beauty of this level of awareness comes the freedom to make a pain-free, happier choice next time. This is precisely what builds strong and loving connections, interdependent relationships, and spiritual resilience.

"Learn to be quiet in the midst of turmoil, for quietness is the end of strife and this is the journey to peace. Look straight at every image that rises to delay you, for the goal is inevitable because it is eternal."

—*A Course in Miracles* (T-12.II.5:5-6)

Much more often, when we notice upset or anger arise, we take a moment to pause and instead reframe our thoughts and release the feelings. The madness has lifted and clarity shines through. We, by the grace of God, look past it, bestowing calm instead of adding to the chaos. No battle necessary. A much friendlier place to be.

As I continue my spiritual journey, I feel I'm being tested. It seems when I make headway, another problem arises. "Can't I get a break?" rolls through my head. "Haven't I suffered enough? Haven't I arrived yet?" Ha ha!

With wisdom I embrace the next thing or another with the thirst of an eager student, excited by every challenge to become all that I can be. On the other hand, I languish in the silly egoic question of "Why me?" I am prompted by Spirit to ask for help, to hear the guidance, to glean the lesson, and no matter how difficult it may seem, I eventually get it. I reap the growth that is almost always delayed by the small mind-running interference. Sometimes it's the same lesson, but a deeper understanding is needed. In a way this is thrilling, too, because there is always room to grow. As a colleague recently voiced, "The desire to learn keeps us young."

As long as we're on earth we ultimately possess the capacity to choose to grow or delay growth. Rest assured, enlightenment is inevitable.

"The word 'inevitable' is fearful to the ego, but joyous to the spirit."

—*A Course in Miracles* (T-4.I.9:10)

Part IV: Tranquil Seas

Chapter 24: Yet Another Clever Disguise

"Would you, for all these meaningless distractions, lay Heaven aside? Your destiny and purpose are far beyond them, in the clean place where littleness does not exist."

—*A Course in Miracles* (T-23.in.4:5-6)

Our travails while trudging this earth are viewed by the ego as sins and by Spirit as mistakes that only need correction. If that is the case then mistakes are just lessons that lead us closer to the truth of our invincibility. A mistake, then, is a clever disguise toward universal oneness and ineffable peace.

One of our biggest barriers to lasting peace is competing with ourselves and our fellow earth travelers, and spinning off from that comes the need to be right, which sends us back into the spiral of pride and dissatisfaction. This reinforces the belief that we are not good enough and others are out to steal our glory. When we are under the lower mind's advisement, now filled with pride that we are better than others, we are robbed of all sense of peace, all while in our defense exclaiming, "But it is a matter of pride!"

Excessive pride, spurred again by the fear that we're somehow defective, demands our small self to be praised, win approval and admiration, get the trophy, and be worshiped. Fame with or without the fortune. This can easily become an obsessive need. We cannot be wrong and must be right at any price lest we lose face. Grandiosity isolates us from others. Have you ever hung on for dear life to an opinion in the midst of a heated conversation, even though it had become obvious that you were wrong? During these battles, often with those we care for, we must feel superior, or else we are viewed as "less than," which can only mean that we are weak, disfavored, and vulnerable.

I continually learn from my adult children. Once during an opinionated exchange with her older brother, Jacinda ended the conversation masterfully. After the ball of debate rallied back and forth for what could have been the Wimbledon championship, she simply stated, "You're probably right." At that, the conversation came to an amicable but abrupt end. Game over.

Detach, Disengage

Be in the world but not of it. Do what you enjoy but carry with you always your connection to Source. It is so simple to bring the present moment into all that you do. Traveling the world, achieving success personally or professionally, wanting more of a good thing—realize that none of this is permanent except the love, joy, and beauty that you experience in that moment, which can never be lost.

Utilize your passions to achieve great things, welcome fun activities, and heal your perceptions of the ailing as you simultaneously heal yourself. Bring harmony and peace wherever you go, protect the innocent by seeing past injustices to the goodness that lies beneath, and enjoy this earth because joy is your natural inheritance. The secret is to remember that these pastimes are not the end-all. They are simply windows that, if welcomed for what they are, will inevitably lead to the everlasting light and security within that is your one Self.

"The Now"

Total
Surrender
Let go completely
Live in the now
Sweet moment
Breathe
See
Hear
Things we may let go by and may
Never see again, . . . feel again, hear,
A million new sensations
Warmth
Touch
Breath
Energy
Now
One foot
Then the other, it seems a struggle
But even this in the present
Is somehow still satisfying
Because it is

It is
Yet joy is found amidst pain when
We shine the light of the present on it
What a mystery
All these long years
The search for peace, contentment,
Happiness
All the time
Wrapped up in this one moment
So simple and so
Elusive
So simple
So slippery
And sometimes unreachable.

Belief, then, is trust, faith, or confidence in a person, concept, or thing. I went to an event last week comprised of a diverse group of women entrepreneurs. One of the speakers, Julia, shared a valuable lesson. Her intriguing lecture outlined the misleading power of belief. She closed her talk with a story. She had served on a think tank, and after coming up with a proposal entailing lengthy steps, her colleagues were not only satisfied with their ingenious result but thrilled with it. This attachment to what they'd worked hard to create made them unwilling to examine it further. However, Julia was getting an intuitive red alert over the weekend. As she investigated this hunch further it struck her in a sudden insight that the steps were perfect but based upon a faulty hypothesis. Unable to deny Julia's logic, the members of the think tank begrudgingly went back to the drawing board.

That reminds me of a comical incident when my sister, daughter, baby granddaughter, and I were driving through Denver years ago to attend a wedding shower. With Pam at the wheel, all of us, very unfamiliar with the area and already running late, were frantically searching for a particular street that was mentioned in the verbal directions. We drove for a long while in circles when it occurred to one of us, "Why are we looking for this street?" The street was mentioned but only as a possible route to reach the destination. Once we let go of our attachment to finding this particular street, which we had bypassed completely, we realized that we were practically on top of our destination. We arrived a little late, embarrassed and a bit frazzled until we saw the humor of it all.

My point is this: Where you put your faith is crucial. It is our beliefs that control us. Be vigilant of the beliefs in which you invest your time, energy, and money. A belief is not a fact. Sometimes it's just another runaway thought. It's important to question your beliefs often and bring them to the light of truth.

It is a well-known fact that a thought becomes a belief when it is repeated over and over again. For example, if you believe that you are always treated unfairly or that wealth only comes to people who have higher education, this will pretty much become your experience. These erroneous beliefs are superimposed onto your world, clouding the truth. Thus the lower mind will selectively gather information that supports the belief while ignoring anything that contradicts it. In my mind this is the opposite of open-minded objectivity and curiosity, dousing the spirit of learning and the understanding that comes with clear vision.

What a world we uncover when we take a step back and examine our beliefs objectively through the eyes of unlimited possibility, turning to the Guide within instead. This requires keeping your finger on the pulse of higher wisdom, inner knowing, and the love and light within. We don't arrive at enlightenment for more than an instant in this realm, yet each decision brings us closer or further away.

At one time or another each of us has felt incomplete, broken, hurt, grief-stricken, lost, and fallible due to the mistakes we've made or what we might classify as just plain bad luck. Yet, it bears repeating: Every perceived error or dilemma can become a stepping stone to peace when we garner the courage to examine it closely and release, reframe, or rebalance it as needed. Every loss can be a journey toward oneness, and every hurt or mistake can become an opportunity for healing when you reach out your heart and hand to your fellow earth travelers, for the essence of who we are cannot be hurt. Have you known someone who lost everything and, in hindsight, concluded that it was the best thing that could have happened for all concerned?

You are worlds beyond this body. We need not get hung up on our perceived defects, but when we do, we have been given the grace to look beyond illusion and remember the truth about who we are beyond bodies, beyond perception, and *beyond belief.*

"When grandeur slips away from you, you have replaced it with something you have made. Perhaps it is the belief in littleness; perhaps it is the belief in grandiosity."

—*A Course in Miracles* (T-9.VIII.7:3-4)

Chapter 25: Steeped in Joy and Devotion

"Today our purpose is to free the world from all the idle thoughts we ever held about it, and about all living things we see upon it. They can not be there. No more can we. For we are in the home our Father set for us, along with them."

—*A Course in Miracles* (W-132.14:1-4)

"We are game-playing, fun-having creatures, we are the otters of the universe. We cannot die, we cannot hurt ourselves any more than illusions on the screen can be hurt. But we can believe we're hurt, in whatever agonizing detail we want. We can believe we're victims, killed and killing, shuddered around by good luck and bad luck. Why are we here? For fun and learning."

—Richard Bach, *Illusions*

Joy and purpose. Our natural state is joy. To realize the joy of eternal oneness, every obstacle becomes a journey to uncovering that joy. In essence this is your purpose, and coming back home equates to coming back to joy, the joy that you are.

It's not that we should be happy or that we deserve to be joyous. It's not by insisting or demanding that we find happiness. Sure, we can fool ourselves, partaking in outside means and influences in the use of mind-altering substances and daring exploits. However, nothing compares to authentic timeless joy. Joy is, in essence, our undeniable indistinguishability. The glue that makes us one with all life.

For example, I went skiing the other day and had one stellar run after the other. I am so grateful to my son Jeremy for reintroducing me to skiing several years ago when he began snowboarding after a fifteen-year hiatus. We have the most fun together. Each of us welcomes a joy that cannot be sourced externally. Perhaps this is because skiing requires that we embrace the present moment. Conversely, I derive great pleasure in skiing solo as I find myself carving my way into what can only be called a meditative zone of tranquility. Usually I am ecstatic if I get just one amazing run in a day.

Everything seemed perfect on this particular day. The snow met my boards with the silkiness of fluffy iced cream, I had the slopes basically to myself, and the visibility went from clear to cloudy to snowy. I enjoy skiing in low light, especially when it is snowing, because it forces me to lean into every non-visual sensation at my disposal—the sounds of the wind whipping past my earlobes and snow crackling under my skis, the taste of cold crisp air passing my lips, the subtle variances of the ice and powder reverberating up through my feet, knees, and hips, stabilizing my descent, and the pungent smell of frozen bark and pine needles. You might say when devoid of clear eyesight, I more easily rely on other senses as I merge reverently with a living, breathing mountain.

Oddly, since I haven't used mind-altering substances in well over thirty years, in the midst of this spectacular day the thought occurred to me that having a drink might enhance the bliss still more! It didn't take but a nanosecond after I recovered from the initial bewilderment that I registered this was none other than the lower mind talking. It is never satisfied with things as they are and will constantly push us over the edge into hardship and distress. At this point I busted out laughing. As I have astonishingly discovered with sobriety, when things are really good it is so much more fulfilling to sink into goodness instead of allowing yourself to be greedily coerced into regrettable indulgences. Take the good times as they come, and when you embrace every moment fully with your whole being, you find it doesn't get any better, for the happiness in life occurs only in the moment you are in right now. Nothing can enhance the now but by fully welcoming it. Having a drink, a drug, or excess of any kind only dulls the senses and robs you of the ecstasy of your natural state of joy.

All we have to do is work through the barriers that keep us from that recognition. We don't have to strive for happiness because our real purpose is to rediscover the joy and oneness that is us. Lester Levenson states that despite the temptation to ride the emotional rollercoaster, our top goal ought to be imperturbability, which aligns perfectly with detaching from desire in the teachings of Buddhism. As such, we become imperturbable, not disturbed by outside events on our path to enlightenment. Outside events or inner turmoil that seem to rock the boat or push our buttons become our measuring stick—either our demise or our salvation—laying out our customized road map, detours and all, to happy destiny.

Blaming the world and fighting feelings of guilt and self-pity are what we bring with us into the physical realm, buying into the small minds' delirium. Rather, it's wiser to dive into and investigate all that does not bring you joy. This sagacious approach will undoubtedly awaken your omnipresent but sleeping liberation. Then we can ask for help once again, choose differently to look beyond the clouds that obscure. A single decision gives access to what some might call Christ vision, and in that instant save ourselves from a lifetime of misery and unearth the light within you and me instead. It's no wonder *A Course in Miracles* refers to this as a holy instant.

This is a newfound freedom to celebrate. No longer do we apply a band-aid of escapism and settle for our small mind's interpretations. In that holy instant you have succeeded in freeing yourself, as well as all living things that have come before or ever will come in the ego's illusory world of time.

Many are lost in the haze of searching for purpose. At some point, unconsciously, we believe we haven't found our life's purpose, convinced we are just not living up to our potential. The feverish search for purpose has a way of squeezing the playfulness out of life. We may ask what our purpose is, and when we discover hidden talents or gifts they begin to emerge through us uniquely. Take the pressure off of finding purpose and instead dedicate yourself to welcoming designs that arise in the moment and let that be your guide.

Our deeper purpose intertwined with our unique talents is to realize our joy and oneness with all life by uncovering and forgiving the lies of the ego. Peace and joy are literally unearthed when we adjust our perceptions. "Help me see this differently" is the call we make for a change in perception and is all that is needed to recover the happiness that you were meant to enjoy.

"For we have found a simple, happy way to leave the world of ambiguity, and to replace our shifting goals and solitary dreams with single purpose and companionship."

—*A Course in Miracles* (W-200.11:5)

We Cannot Be Hurt

"If you will listen to His Voice you will know that you cannot either hurt or be hurt, and that many need your blessing to help them hear this for themselves."

—*A Course in Miracles* (T-6.I.19:2)

The essence of who we really are cannot be hurt. Our thoughts and beliefs about traumatic events that are in the past or to come in our imagination are used as weapons, which keep us churning in the hopeless, helpless, problem-focused world of ego. We cannot be hurt, as *A Course in Miracles* emphasizes, for our spirit never dies. We can only think we are hurt by recycling the past over and over again and projecting it onto the future. It is essentially our thinking that seems to destroy or damage us. We are continually being called to dive into, process, and let go with our mind's eye wide open.

The key concept is for-giveness—to give it up to a power greater than our small selves—only then will it be transformed into the one thing that is eternal, the light of love. Our redirected belief dawns a new way of looking at things, a new perception. There is no dearth of grace and goodwill, for we are steeped in love. Love heals all, and we are light-beings temporarily mistaking ourselves as separate bodies.

Our little escapades on earth, our lessons if you will, bring us back home to the knowledge that nothing can take that love away, especially past memories skewed by the misinterpretations of the small mind. The ego gains strength by wallowing in preoccupation with the past. The chorus that requires examining and letting go sounds a lot like I am a victim, I have been unfairly treated, I am damaged, broken, or hurt.

In our opening quote Richard compares us to the otters of the universe, and, like otters, we are excitable, fun-loving, spirited creatures who love to express ourselves. Otters are often referred to as loyal and honest animals. In the light of oneness, we are also caring and authentic beings. Otters are instinctively adept at motivating the bevy and need to be in an environment where they can connect and be a part of the whole. Deep inside this is what we are craving too.

How is the otter analogy juxtaposed against the ego's delusion of wrong-mindedness? Ego wants to be separate. Despises oneness. It will lie to protect itself and turn against the flock in a moment of need. It is suspicious of others and wants to get something or take it away so as to make itself stronger, which truly only weakens it. Yes, the ego is immersed in the murky waters of single-minded greed.

All of the discipline dedicated to freeing ourselves, on top of the constant state of vigilance regarding the negative thoughts of the ego, can be, well, consuming, and we frequently forget our purpose, which is to live as best and joyously as we can close to Source instead of constantly on the lookout for ego. As it happens, it is an art to recognize imbalance to then ask for help, hear the guidance, and trust it, thus becoming a master at returning to bliss. This is the formula back to the fun and happiness that is not only possible in this world but is also our calling. Imagine the freedom you'd feel if you knew at the deepest level that you are safe—a secure part of the whole and loved beyond your wildest dreams. You could finally welcome your otter-like nature. Your oneness with all, the bevy of love and light that is you. The obstacles we encounter on earth are meant to escort us back to center. To realize the joy of eternal oneness, every obstacle becomes your instrumentality.

The revelation within the process of undoing the ego is a hidden inner brilliance as we get better at recognizing the ploys of the lower mind. We are called to dive into perceived problems, past trauma, and future fears, then give them up to

Spirit, like a balloon rising into divinity, and in a holy instant find ourselves back where we belong—in the company of devoted lighthearted oneness.

While attending to earthly tasks, I invite you to prioritize joy. Make your sole purpose to discover perfect peace as you uncover and let go of wrong-mindedness.

We could be otter-like, too, happily coming back to center as needed. Playful, devoted creatures, frequently seen sliding down muddy riverbanks or burrowing through new-fallen snow. That could be you and me. Why not?

"He will go before you making straight your path, and leaving in your way no stones to trip on, and no obstacles to bar your way. Nothing you need will be denied you. Not one seeming difficulty but will melt away before you reach it. You need take thought for nothing, careless of everything except the only purpose that you would fulfill."

—*A Course in Miracles* (T-20.IV.8:5-8)

Chapter 26: Life Is Pretty Amazing

"Everything in this world is little because it is a world made out of littleness, in the strange belief that littleness can content you. When you strive for anything in this world in the belief that it will bring you peace, you are belittling yourself and blinding yourself to glory."

—*A Course in Miracles* (T-15.III.1:5-6)

Billy never left. It was only my mistaken belief that we could be separated that prolonged my desperate need to reunite with him. For many years following Billy's short earth walk mournfulness seeped into every corner of my existence. In my despair I'd abandoned an ancient truth. He need not call me because the light that unifies us has never gone out. We are one and cannot be separated, and it is this same love that joins you and me and all who have ever walked this earth.

The horrors that you and I believe we've endured were only a dream. And we wake up by moving through the cherished and tragic stories, erroneous beliefs, turbulent emotions, and imbalances of any memory that surfaces in the moment until we finally come to rest where we were always perfectly innocent, whole, and secure.

"Today I wake with joy, expecting but the happy things of God to come to me. I ask but them to come, ... And I will ask for only joyous things the instant I accept my holiness.

For what would be the use of pain to me, what purpose would my suffering fulfill, and how would grief and loss avail me . . . ?"

—*A Course in Miracles* (W-285.1:1-4)

Waking with joy sounds a bit Pollyannaish. Still, I've found that today we can wake with joy, expecting the happy things of Universal Love to come to us because when we stop, pause, and look beyond the chaos, life is pretty amazing. Authentic joy comes easier, especially after you've done so much thus far at lightening your heavy load and have become versed in welcoming every external challenge and every inner disturbance that shows up with honesty and courage.

"This is the way in which time is exchanged for eternity."

—*A Course in Miracles* (T-5.VI.12:2)

"There is no hurry now, for you are using time for its intended purpose."

—*A Course in Miracles* (W-rIV.in.7:3)

When I say "life," that doesn't mean the time we spend on earth, which is at best a consuming distraction that, with God's help, can become valuable lessons in spiritual unity and growth and, at worst, is really just a brief nightmare. The essence of life depicts a very different reality: We are as one eternal beautiful light of love, loved, and loving that extends in peace beyond space and time.

Life is forever beautiful, and while on earth most of us only experience glimpses of this amazing continuum called life. The closest we come is when we are immersed in the present moment—meditation, a hike in nature, a stunning sunset. Over the course of many years there has been a shift from living my days on earth with guilt and blame to living with love and integrity, one light-being exchange at a time.

When you look beyond illusion life is pretty amazing. Why? Because the world we think we inhabit is actually a misperception. This is not your life, and what you're experiencing is many opportunities disguised as problems to dive into and through so you can come back to the realization that you are not form but spirit. This earthly life is merely a set of obstacles to realizing the truth of your immortality and eternal peace, not to be denied but investigated and explored until you discover that it was all just a dream—a spiritual being having a human experience.

Yes, life is pretty amazing. Our earth jaunt is an unnecessary process that necessitates following the whims of the ego. It is a process of remembering that we are a part of something bigger than that which seems to take form and die. A celestial nudge designed to arouse within you a peace beyond belief.

Our brief excursions on earth are solely an exercise sharpening our skills to recollect our everlasting shared oneness. In essence we are here to undo the belief in ego and unlearn its teachings. We are essentially coming back to a place within that we never left.

The concept of time only clouds our real life. Yet it is in a tiny segment of time that a world of brilliance opens before us. That tiny crack is this now. Childlike joy and authenticity, freedom to be, like an infant exploring their world, we are filled with pure curiosity and pleasure.

Take this now to notice the air passing your nostrils, follow the flight of a butterfly, or lay back on the grass and gaze at the clouds or the astounding view when you summit a mountain. Listen to the rain with every fiber of your being or hear the snow falling as you tune in more and more.

None of these ineffable pleasures can be experienced outside the now. Have you ever noticed how your glands secrete saliva just before you bite into a pickle or how you absorb the vitality of the earth through your sandals that cradle your feet as you stroll down a path? Can you smell the heady perfume of a horse pasture or experience the lavish negative ions pouring through you near a gushing waterfall? These are all moments out of time that give a glimpse of the paradise that we never left because heaven lies forever within us.

Bliss is found in this perfect now! The buoyant, gravity-defying sensation while swimming. The cool squishy mud between your toes at the edge of a lake and the fishy smell that permeates the air. A good novelist enraptures you with her writing because she is good at one thing—painting a picture with words where every sensation, every nuance, every subtle, hue, tone, and shade of color is described in such detail that you are there in that moment. And who is to say you are not?

Why not be there in the instant that lies before you? For every now you touch brings you closer to authentic freedom, closer to enlightenment. Inner unshakable peace exists now. A single second holds within it the realization that you were always here. The entirety of perfect peace is now.

"Such is the meeting place we try today to find and rest in, for the peace of God is where your Self, His Son, is waiting now to meet Itself again, and be as one."

—*A Course in Miracles* (W-92.9:3)

When we begin to string more of these nows together we're that much closer, and yet it only takes one instant to reach nirvana. Enlightenment is not a destination—it is a realization! We may learn to experience bliss even when it comes to our attention that our taxes are due and chores are calling. How? By tuning into the visceral tension mounting between the upper back, neck, and shoulder blades, bringing our awareness to the discomfort and giving it space to be for a minute or two. Then, the tension dissolves, and we will be more likely to just take the necessary action rather than mulling it over or making it into another "woe is me" story. We are moved from a place of calm rather than panic-driven reactivity. This yields less procrastination and more freedom. We just heightened our access to the universal vibration of ease and opened the door to a peace beyond belief.

Mind you, when you embrace and release the emotion or examine and reframe the thought, it begs the question, "Where do they go?" It is my understanding that it is the same divine alchemy that springs forth through the act of forgiving, forgiving what we judge now, allowing Spirit to transform it into love and light. Each time you identify and let go of a discursive thought or an unsettling emotion you strengthen your spiritual resilience and lift the veil between your mistaken beliefs and peace.

In this way you are the filter, filtering out illusion so you can experience real joy and happiness. The bliss that was there all along. It was just hidden by the debris in the frantic thoughts manufactured by the small mind.

"I Am"

Freedom
Now
Color
Balance
Clarity
The Warmth of the Sun
The Kiss of a Breeze
The Mystery of the Wild
The Depth of Granite
The Innocence of a Child

Clarity
Balance
Color
Now
Freedom

Chapter 27: Mastering the River of Life

"The Holy Spirit wants only this, for sharing the Father's Love for His Son, He seeks to remove all guilt from his mind that he may remember his Father in peace. Peace and guilt are antithetical, and the Father can be remembered only in peace."

—*A Course in Miracles* (T-13.I.1:1-3)

The days that I struggle and find myself frustrated indicate that I've decided to go it alone, stuck like glue to my rigid plans, and shifted back into autopilot once again. I arrogantly believe that I know what is best and don't need divine guidance. It's simple: I am clearly unplugged from my higher all-knowing Teacher. I am reminded this is a minute-by-minute journey, and remembering I know nothing is my greatest gateway. Recalling this keeps me humble and makes it so much easier to release my attachment to beliefs in which I can become stubbornly invested. Every moment is a new opportunity no matter how it shows up, a divine opportunity to access the peace that unfolds effortlessly when I pause, take a step back, and choose to look beyond my thwarted perceptions. I have discovered enlightened peace and pure happiness in the ordinary moments—one holy instant at a time.

The days my mind is eased into divine flow are due to unleashing what I call my spiritual sweet spot. The delicious moments when I give my entire will to God, plan nothing, and ask for direction in the moment. Trusting. When I lean into ease, allowing myself to move in the direction that I am being guided, it is as if I'm walking on clouds and everything unfolds before me in ways I could not have imagined. So often fear and resistance crop up at first. These emotions can shut down the flow in a second. However, instead of letting that stop me I recognize fear as energy passing through and let it go, which ironically strengthens my sacred connection and sense of security.

Every time I listen and obey there is a knowing within me, whether a subtle inner urging or a billboard in my mind's eye pointing the way. Almost every time it makes no logical sense, yet when I act from faith it is always revealed that it was the perfect next right step. I end up in a place of tranquility and lightness without struggle, strain, and forcing with which the ego used to control me. I'm no doubt in my infancy on this sacred walk and do my best to nurture this spiritual sweet spot by bringing more trust and flow into my every waking moment.

Wrong-minded stories roll around in my head with one difference. I recognize them, relinquish my fascination with them, and let them pass through more quickly. And yet the small mind continues to lure me away with two favorite tactics: guilt and blame. Like ping pong it uses one to distract me and then the other. Funny how I've learned I am the one keeping the ball in play. With a simple request, Source reveals these untruths. Now when the seemingly immovable boulder of guilt shows up I ask for the courage to see it for what it is and dispel it, for enlightenment happens in these ordinary moments. Believing I am unworthy and deserve punishment, as in the legend of Sisyphus, I drag my self-made boulder up a hill into the depths of Hades needlessly. That's when I exercise free will to hold onto and cling to this boulder as much as I do, and when I do this earnestly, after about ninety seconds it gets tiring and sometimes painful. That's when I ask myself if I can just let it go and give it up to God. A weight is lifted as I release it, as if I held a pebble of guilt in my hand and let it tumble to the ground. It dawns on me again that trying to lug heavy emotion around keeps me from living as I was meant to live, in peace.

It serves no one to hang on to the ludicrous belief that you deserve condemnation. You are estimable of quite the opposite, an innocent and beloved child of God. At this point in my heart I envision the invulnerability of the supposed injured party whom I thought I could harm. They remain untouched, invincible, pure light and love. Damning yourself doesn't help you or them. If so moved, make amends as you let the shame and guilt go. Mistakes hold within them great learning. The act of admitting a mistake extends a curative olive branch, restoring the bridge of oneness to your fellow travelers. Glean the wisdom bestowed and give yourself permission to receive the grace you've been given.

In the same respect, when I catch myself launching into stories of blame and watch in horror as I attempt to hurl this heavy finger-pointing rock, which requires enormous energy, I can decide to ask to see this differently, giving myself permission to sink into the feelings of victimization, and usually in less than two minutes I am able to drop the rock of blame too. After all, it only hinders me to carry the burden of blame and shame.

It's a journey. I've come to realize both of my children have given me more grace around my erratic behaviors than I've given myself. God is helping me with higher Self-love and self-forgiveness too.

Today I have become capable of more happiness than I ever thought possible betwixt and between the exposed rocks of upset that surely surface in this realm. As the act of shining light on my mistaken perceptions erodes away lies, what remains is pure, unadulterated, childlike glee.

There are fewer boulders, rocks, and sludge with each excavation and more joy that I may not have had the fortune to delight in during my tumultuous upbringing. Now my earth walk is less like trudging unfathomable misery and a lot more like fielding the next upset with alacrity.

I am blessed to enjoy a purposeful, passion-filled career that stirs great satisfaction, giving way to a deep affection for my profession, working hand in hand with my inner Teacher to help others access the all-knowing Guide within. Add the amazing growth-stirring relationships with family, friends, pets, and even those whom I've not yet met, playing like a child with complete abandon toward wherever my heart and soul lead me. I envision the essence of life in every snowflake, every dewdrop, every molecule of air, and every branch on a tree while skiing, snowshoeing, laughing with friends, soaking in hot mineral springs, stargazing in the desert, swimming in oceans, jogging on beaches, and hiking up mountains. I take in the incredible, mind-blowing wonders of nature, floating down the rivers of my authentic, glowing, fun-having immortal life.

Row, row, rowing my boat gently down the stream with God at the helm, merrily, merrily, merrily at one with all life—including you. And as one, we transcend our world of misery into a peace beyond belief, for life on earth is but a dream.

In gratitude for all of this and all that shows up.

"Now is there silence all around the world. Now is there stillness where before there was a frantic rush of thoughts that made no sense. Now is there tranquil light across the face of earth, made quiet in a dreamless sleep."

—*A Course in Miracles* (W-198.11:1-3)

Bibliography

Bach, R. (1989). *Illusions: The Adventures of a Reluctant Messiah.* Dell.

Bach, R. (1998). *There's No Such Place as Far Away.* Delta.

Dwoskin, H. (2003). *The Sedona Method: Your Key to Lasting Happiness, Success, Peace and Emotional Well-being.* Sedona Press.

Hay, L. (1984). *You Can Heal Your Life.* Hay House LLC.

Jampolsky, G. (1979). *Love is Letting Go of Fear.* Celestial Arts.

Katie, B. (2003). *Loving What Is: Four Questions That Can Change Your Life.* Three Rivers Press.

Levenson, L. (2003). *The Ultimate Truth (About Love & Happiness): A Handbook to Life.* Lawrence Crane Enterprises.

Schucman, H. (2008). *A Course in Miracles: Combined Volume.* Foundation for Inner Peace.

W., B. (1939). *Alcoholics Anonymous: The Big Book.* Ixia Press.

No author. (1981). *Al-Anon's Twelve Steps & Twelve Traditions.* Al Anon Family Group Headquarter.

About the Author

Donna Lee Humble, founder of bioSynergy Better Health, and author of *Seek Not for Love*, is a Certified Lifestyle & Wellness Coach and Holistic Health Practitioner, specializing in frequency specific detoxification via computerized bioenergetic testing. She is a Spiritual Teacher, Inspirational Speaker, Emotional Release Expert, creator of the *Higher Self Care* series, and contributing author to various publications, including Mind Body Soul magazine. Donna Lee's passion for holistic wellness has spearheaded the creation of workshops and personalized holistic wellness coaching programs. She is celebrated locally and nationwide for empowering you to embrace your passion, purpose, and peace naturally. Having overcome a plethora of emotional trauma and physical ailments through natural means, she has joyfully served thousands of proactive holistic-minded women and men as they refine their better health, emotional wellness and spiritual connection since 2001.

Donna Lee resides in the heart of the Rocky Mountains of Colorado. She finds great pleasure in traveling to the beach and the desert as often as possible. A professional wildlife watercolor artist, she enjoys painting, hiking in nature, yoga, tennis, river rafting, skiing, and spending quality time with her husband, adult children, niece and nephews, and grandchildren whenever possible.

To learn more about Donna Lee Humble and her practice, she may be contacted via:

Donna Lee Humble
812 Grand Ave., Suite 218
Glenwood Springs, CO 81601
970-274-1680

Visit www.donnaleehumble.com to access Donna Lee's books, the free guide, YouTube videos, blogs, and her most popular podcast episode.

www.ingramcontent.com/pod-product-compliance
Lightning Source LLC
Chambersburg PA
CBHW060554080526
44585CB00013B/554